"If you're trying to wrap your head around the rapidly expanding world of botanical beers, there's no better place to start than the extensive experiments in *Against All Hops*. It's not a rejection of hops, but a warm embrace of just about everything else."

—RANDY MOSHER, author of *Radical Brewing, Tasting Beer, Mastering Homebrew* and *Beer for All Seasons*

"Butch throws all convention out the window on brewing beer with hops and embellishes the use of herbs and spices . . . Nothing is off limits for the gruit. *Against All Hops* is a fun must-read for all practitioners of brewing anything other than hop based brews, be they witches or just interested brewers."

—TOD MOTT, co-founder, Tributary Brewing Company

"These beautiful ideas begin to uncover the whole world of beers which we have tragically lost from our human consciousness. The stagnant, monopolistic and excessive use of hops substituting for creativity in beer is hereby threatened! Long live the revolution!"

—BRIAN HUNT, founder, Moonlight Brewing Company

"A fascinating and mouthwatering look at the multiple alternatives to hops in beer that our ancestors knew all about and we have almost forgotten. You'll put this book down not just wanting to drink the beers described inside, but brew them yourself."

—MARTYN CORNELL, beer historian, author and blogger at Zythophile.co.uk

AGAiNST ALL HOPS

TECHNiQUES AND PHiLOSOPHY FOR CREATiNG EXTRAORDiNARY BOTANiCAL BEERS

Butch Heilshorn CO-FOUNDER OF EARTH EAGLE BREWiNGS

PAGE STREET
PUBLISHING CO.

PAGE STREET
PUBLISHING CO.

First published in 2017 by

Page Street Publishing Co.

27 Congress Street, Suite 105

Salem, MA 01970

www.pagestreetpublishing.com

Distributed by Macmillan, sales in Canada by The Canadian Manda Group.

21 20 19 18 17   1 2 3 4 5

ISBN-13: 978-1-62414-379-3

ISBN-10: 1-62414-379-2

Library of Congress Control Number: 2017936162

Cover and book design by Page Street Publishing Co.

Photography by James Jay Fortin

Printed and bound in China

FOR ALL OF THE INTREPID IMBIBERS
WHO HELP EARTH EAGLE FLY.

CONTENTS

EXHILARATION   37

Based on a combination of herbs thought to be the holy trinity of ancient gruit beer, this re-creation yields a delicious assortment of bready, spicy and citrusy flavors that will dazzle your palate.

BLOOMERS   43

Brewing with fresh local flowers is an incredible way to create a liquid snapshot of a particular time and place. This Belgian-esque light beer presents earthy, spicy and, yes, flowery notes that will delight.

CHAGA GROOVE   51

This dark, mysterious brew employs maple sap in lieu of water as well as a fungus reputed to be a favorite of Siberian shamans. Root, spice and herbal notes yield to mellow smoke and roast for a warming and most unusual quaff.

MONKEY WEED   57

A tart beer with invasive plants and without souring bacteria? Ya betcha! Japanese knotweed is one of many invasive species plaguing the United States and benefiting creative brewers. Berry, floral and almost lemonade-like, this gose-like beer is an easy summer classic.

BLACK ADDER   63

This milk stout/gruit hybrid features a bit of hops as well two other flavorful herbs. We love our dark beers during the cold months, and this array of roasty, slightly sweet chocolate flavors combined with a whiff of licorice is a tasty winter warmer.

POP! IPA   69

There are a host of herbs that play well with hops, particularly poplar buds. Invigoratingly herbal and minty citrus, this shines new light on where India pale ales (IPAs) can go.

CHINESE ROCK 75

The first beer we ever brewed, a big burley barley wine gruit and not a hop in sight. Later versions featured additional off-the-wall ingredients taking the big beer concept into some very tasty and complex territory.

GALLOWS HARVEST 81

We brew lots of history-influenced beers, some of which come from arcane journals and texts unearthed by a history professor friend of ours. This compelling Halloween beer is based on one of his finds, with toffee malt-based flavors and light spice, faint squash and tart fruit notes.

DRAKONIA 89

Too much of anything is often a bad thing, and ancient beer ingredients are no exception. This recipe features mandrake, a root with a mysterious history. Drakonia is a good introductory gruit; unusual flavors abound in this balanced, slightly sweet amber.

PORTER COCHON 95

Meat beers? Who knew! Used sparingly, rather than turning beer into a broth or soup, meat (here, smoked pig heads) adds a wonderful smoky and savory dimension to this delicious robust porter base.

CONNIE FERALE 103

Coniferous tree parts in beer not only taste good, they're good for you! These ancient and worldly ingredients come together in this hop-less black IPA base that presents delightfully bright, citrusy and new-growth evergreen notes. No Christmas tree drinking here.

BIRTHDAY BOY 109

Can you really capture a season in a bottle? This golden, light-yet-flavorful brew is just that: spring in a bottle or tank or keg. Foraged herbs provide wonderful earthy forest base notes and tart piney-pepper top notes, with room left over for lovely yeast esters.

CONTINUING THE ADVENTURE 115

We've presented just a tiny selection of the hundreds of plants that can be used in brewing. I suspect there are even more out there waiting to be discovered—or rediscovered. Here are more in-depth suggestions regarding herb use and the deepening of relationships with our magnificent brewing partners.

PREFACE

Are you a home brewer who's tiring of the usual suspects, cycling through the same styles and flavors every other home brewer is perfecting? Are you a professional brewer who's cranking through the same catalog of beers year after year, just adding more hops with each rotation? There might be a bit of salvation here for you.

Maybe you own a brewery and you're wondering what you're going to do when you can't find the hops you need or what to do if this giant hop-bubble ever bursts? Perhaps you're a seasoned imbiber who's starting to wither on the hop bine, craving a new beer experience? This book should give you some cause for pause.

This book was written with experienced all-grain and professional brewers in mind. Gearing up for your first brew day? I found Charlie Papzian's book, *The Complete Joy of Home Brewing*, quite helpful in explaining the basic brewing concepts that are not covered here.

My brother-in-law Alex McDonald and I own and operate Earth Eagle Brewings, a five-barrel brewpub in Portsmouth, New Hampshire. Like any successful brewery, we brew hop-forward beers and like many current craft beer consumers, we are both avowed hop-heads. But creating yet another India pale ale (IPA) was not the motivating force behind our decision to brew. Rather, it was our quest for an ancient hop-less ale called "gruit." Since opening in 2012, we have been doing what no other brewery in the world does—regularly brewing and selling beers that use herbs other than hops to bitter, preserve and flavor.

From April to October, most of the herbs we use grow wild within a 50-mile (80-km) radius of our brewpub. We employ a forager who explores the local forests, fields, mountains and coastal areas to sustainably harvest roots, flowers, leaves, fruits, barks and branches—mushrooms and seaweed too. We take great satisfaction in reinterpreting stouts and sours, pales and porters, rauchbiers and wheat wines, sahtis and weissbiers by using little or no hops; transforming common brews into gruit. During our seven month foraging season, each gruit we brew is an authentic expression of time and place, our unique locale, our particular terroir. There are many brewers out there who believe as I do, that such expressions of time and place are the future of beer. While its future is unknown, gruit is undeniably the history of beer.

ON THE SPECTRUM

Brewing occurs on a spectrum between science and art, between the technician and the artist, the objective and the subjective. Every brewer is on this spectrum somewhere, whether by personality, philosophy and/or brewing style. Most likely it's all of the above, as well as brewing circumstances—being a pro-brewer comes with a lot more strings attached than being a home brewer does!

The science end is all about the numbers, and brewers execute a series of tasks which utilize these numbers. They drive technologies designed to gain more control of the various chemical and thermal systems involved—with the goal of repetition. Variables need to be eliminated as much as possible so that outcomes are predictable and the given beer can be perfectly replicated.

The art side is about intuition and expression—magic even. Brewers are a vessel through which a particular alchemy happens. Chance and circumstance are embraced rather than chased away. Here, it's less about controlling systems and more about cooperating with, even surrendering to, them. Repetition is not the goal, but rather the experimentation, exploration and innovation of brewing. The objective is new and unexpected beer; something that moves brewer and drinker alike to a deeper understanding and appreciation for what beer can be.

So, full disclosure: My spot on the spectrum is as close to the art side as one can be—and still successfully brew quality beer. I'm not a numbers guy but I can use them when I have to. I am eternally grateful for those in my organization and in the industry who are numbers people! I am also not an expert in brewing nor in herbalism—but I have been an active student of both for several years. As the late Zen Master Shunryu Suzuki said, "In the beginner's mind there are many possibilities, but in the expert's there are few." Rather than a dogmatic treatise on brewing, the premise for this book was something along the lines of, "Hey, we're doing some cool stuff, people like it, check it out!"

I heartily invite you, fellow brewers and beer aficionados, to break out of that admittedly wondrous hop box. Discover a vibrant and delicious new world of brewing that's straight from the past, and a world with so many possibilities that you'll spend a lifetime exploring them.

BACK TO THE FUTURE

Beer is old. Some archeologists believe that mankind stumbled upon that first ferment 30,000 years ago. The first hard evidence we have is 7,000 years old and involved the Sumerians, who settled in the Mesopotamian plains (modern-day Iran) and enjoyed a robust beer culture. There is also evidence that a neolithic brew was being enjoyed in China around this time too. Research by Travis Rupp at the University of Colorado indicates that the Sumerians eventually taught the Egyptians to brew, who then taught the Greeks, who taught the Romans who (and the theory starts to fray here) then taught the "savage tribes of Britain and northern Europe." Regardless of who taught who, these early brews contained all manner of fruits, flowers, roots, barks, leaves and buds, largely derived from the brewster's geographic location. Hops? Not so much.

More than 7,000 years of beer, and hops start to become a major player in roughly 1500 AD, which points to at least 5,500 years of non-hopped brewing, almost 80 percent of the history of beer. Well, what were we putting in our beer for 55 centuries? This is the question that nudged me from being a beer drinker to a beer maker. What a wondrous, voluminous, fecund chunk of our human heritage to ponder! The answer: gruit.

Gruit is Old German for "herb," with Old German being the first form of the German language that came into use between roughly 500 to 1050 AD. Through the fifteenth and sixteenth centuries, the meaning of gruit had morphed from the singular herb to the plural herbs, specifically a blend of different plants used in the bittering and flavoring of ale. Fast-forward 500 years and we come to the current meaning, which is defined by a single herb, or rather the lack of it: hops. Gruit has come to mean a category or classification of ale containing little or no hops. But much, much more on that later.

From the fifteenth to the seventeenth century in England, the terms "beer" and "ale" both referred to fermented grain beverages. The difference was that ale did not contain hops and beer did. The advent of this hoppy beverage caused a lot of strife in Europe. For a time, some countries actually had laws against the use of hops to protect what had become a lucrative beer-herb trade. Eventually the tides changed and the use of herbs other than hops became illegal in some places. In 1516, Germany instituted its beer purity law, the *Reinheitsgebot*, setting forth a strict formula consisting of only water, malt and hops. Yeast was by default part of this formula but it was not formally "discovered" until almost 300 years later. By the eighteenth century, virtually all of these fermented grain beverages contained hops, so the terms ale and beer became interchangeable [Peter Mathias, *The Brewing Industry in England*, Cambridge University Press, 1959].

THE ORIGINAL HOME BREWERS

> *"The classic tribal 'brewery' was a group of women sitting in a circle, chewing grains and spitting them into a pot to form a fermentable mass. Some ambient yeast blows in and infects the stuff, you put it away for a while, and bingo, you've got beer."*
>
> —Alan Eames

For that great span of time where gruit beer was the norm, and for some of the time hops came into vogue, women brewed the beer; men just drank it. Brewing was not something novel or remotely special—it was another of the many household chores women performed. Throughout the world, from that first fermentation to roughly the 1400s, the matriarch of the family and/or her female designees would have foraged for, and later grown, their own grains and herbs. They traded with other households and eventually farmers, often extra beer for grain. Brewsters or alewives, as female brewers were called, provided this liquid food stuff to their families and later to family-owned taverns. Single women sold beer too, some of them were known as "cunning folk": folk-healers or witches. Just as fermented beverages have a rich and varied history throughout time and all over the world, so do folk-healers.

Some researchers, such as Jane Peyton and Alan Eames, have concluded that much of pop-culture witch-lore stems from medieval brewster practices. Brewsters boiled and fermented in those black copper cauldrons, kept cats to control the vermin attracted by the grains and would hang a broom, also known as an ale stake, above their door advertising that they had extra beer available, a practice dating back to Roman Britain. The term "boiling" often referred to the process of fermentation, specifically the vigorous off-gassing of CO_2. Since no one knew about yeast, this boiling was regarded as magical, a power that the brewster seemed to possess. And those tall black pointy hats? They were worn so thirsty townsfolk could identify brewsters easily at busy street markets.

These original home brewers, regardless of what country they lived in or what they were called, cultivated an intimate knowledge of their local plants and mushrooms. Some of them were also the first health care providers, as well as the keepers of nature-based spirituality that guided all their practices. These three areas—nutrition, healing and spirituality—blended when beer was used as a vehicle to ingest herbs, drawing upon the healing powers of Mother Earth. Clearly this knowledge was not so much in the service of tasty beer as it was for the health of the village, at least initially. Some of the beers they made were not only alcoholic, but with the addition of certain mushrooms or plants like mandrake or henbane, were narcotic and psychotropic too. Such brews were consumed (by village inhabitants) during certain rituals and to celebrate special occasions.

As organized religion began to take hold throughout the world, folk-healers were seen as spiritual competitors and thus were marginalized and demonized. Christianity co-opted much of their earth-based belief systems and practices with male-centric reinterpretations. Physicians and surgeons began to organize into guilds and took control of health care, condemning cunning folk as charlatans and hucksters. Men with a nose for profit wrested brewing from the hearth, the realm of "unskilled" and low caste women, and thrust it into ever-more efficient collectives and later factories, the realm of skilled men. They regulated the burgeoning industry with an ever-changing series of laws and decrees from both municipal and religious "authorities"—all men.

A series of political, religious and economic changes in the 16th and 17th century Europe, particularly the Protestant Reformation, resulted in a profound shift in brewing practice. Stimulating gruit herbs were increasingly cast as dangerous adulterants, and the use of depressive (and cheaper) hops were encouraged and eventually embraced. During this same time period, the persecution of witches became a social phenomenon, and while there's no direct evidence of these women being killed while they were brewing, many find the timing compelling. Alan Eames described it as "a suppression of women and all things feminine." Dick Cantwell, in the seminal *Oxford Companion to Beer*, reported that "puritanical interdictions against the use in beer of substances putatively psychotropic and aphrodisiacal, as well as the condemnation of the practices of brewsters as tantamount to witchcraft, helped hasten the general discontinuation of the production and use of gruit."

BEGINNING OF THE END

When humanity began to farm instead of gather (some say so that they could have a regular supply of brewing ingredients) and raise livestock rather than hunt, many people began to settle together rather than roam. In this emerging lifestyle, growing degrees of specialization began to occur amongst the inhabitants. The average resident needed to know less and less about how to provide for themselves. You could barter with a neighbor or just go to the market place for goods and services. Eventually some villages became towns, and some towns became cities with significant populations, and currency came to replace the barter system and work force specialization continued. Urbanites could specialize in brick-laying, metal smithing or brewing and pay other "professionals" for the other goods and services they needed.

In Europe, an unfortunate consequence of this "civilizing" was that water in highly populated urban regions became too contaminated to drink. Rivers and streams were utilized as sewer systems that flushed away all manner of waste downstream, populating the water with hearty strains of hostile bacteria. While their grasp of science was limited, medieval people realized that the brewing process somehow made water wholesome again, so everyone drank beer, from Grandpa and Grandma to the kids.

While there are ruins of ancient, relatively large-scale breweries in Egypt and other sites in the Middle East, it is thought that they were in the service of temples and that this beer was consumed ritualistically during religious events and festivals. Church and state being one and the same at that time, this beer is also thought to have been the fuel and compensation for the building of the great pyramids. It would be centuries before large breweries began to appear in the West, once again spurred on by organized religion.

Starting in fourth-century Europe, some men left society and started living communally in order to devote themselves to prayer—brewsters were not invited. These pious devotees needed their beer and thus began the legacy of men, specifically monks, brewing beer for each other in monasteries, some of which housed more than 100 monks. Brewing for this many people was a whole new scale of production, something a cauldron or two was not going to be able to handle. And, like most brewers, the monks often had extra beer available, beer that would go bad if it sat around for too long. Like the brewsters before them, they quickly realized that selling this excess was a lucrative form of income, something that non-religious men began to take note of too.

While a small number of women were certainly involved in some of these larger-scale breweries, the dawn of the industrial revolution in the early 1800s marked the final death knell for the brewster and domestic brewing in Europe and America. Production methods for goods and commodities evolved from hand methods to machines and eventually the factories. The textile industry's use of steam power was a giant step, and large breweries quickly followed suit. Advancements in chemical manufacturing also brought methods to standardize brewing practices and exert a level of quality control, specifically the thermometer and the hydrometer. Later advances in storage, specifically refrigeration, as well as transportation in the form of railroads, served to foster yet another quantum leap in the growth of the commercial beer industry.

WAS IT ALL FOR THE BEST?

When thirst and hunger became a business, food production became industrialized. When disease became a business, health care became industrialized. Vast sums of money are being made at every step, from every aspect of these necessities that allow us to survive, if only marginally. Even spirituality wasn't safe! Co-opted by "organized religion," our relationship with the supernatural has been twisted into vast revenue-generating schemes the world over.

Beer has not been immune. Something profound happened when it began to be manufactured and sold in ginormous quantities. An ever-growing list of "do's" and an even bigger list of "don'ts" was established in the name of consistency, systemization, efficiency, shelf-life and ultimately, the bottom line: profitability. In fairly short order, beer, in all its small-batched regional glory, was replaced by one style almost the world over, mass-produced by a few international conglomerates. Over the last hundred years or so, we have grown thoroughly accustomed to this industrial beer. Most of the drinking public have no clue about the rich and varied history of this yellow fizzy homogenized stuff, no clue beyond what comes from vast football fields of machinery, circuitry and computers. But that, thank Bacchus, is changing.

BACK TO THE FUTURE

And here we are in the midst of the Craft Beer Revolution, a phenomenon that began with some hiccups in the United States in the 1980s. There are more breweries now than there were before Prohibition, and more opening every day. The market share of corporate lager is on the wane while craft beer skyrockets—but eight or nine beers out of every ten sold are still of the fizzy yellow factory persuasion. Another curious fact: Most of these new breweries producing "craft," "artisanal" or "handmade" beer are getting their malt and hops and yeast from the same handful of companies—to make the same styles of beer!

Thankfully, there is a growing legion of new brewers who are eschewing the generic corporate malt/yeast/hops truck and are instead utilizing more local sources for their raw materials. They are re-discovering the merits of what is available in their particular geographic areas in lieu of stuff shipped from across the country or across the world. Their communities are starting to appreciate the resulting economic benefits of keeping money local by supporting regional farmers, foragers, maltsters and hop growers. These brewers are unplugging from corporate group-think and reclaiming vital relationships with each other and the natural world in which we live. Oh, and they are making some damn tasty beer too!

BREWING PARTNERS

Let's take a step back from the history and ponder the obvious facts: Brewing is a completely plant-dependent endeavor. From grain, the base of all beer, to the herbs which bitter, preserve and flavor all beer, to the yeast we employ to ferment sugar into alcohol, plants are more than mere ingredients in a recipe—they are our partners in the craft. Plants as *partners?* For us, this can be a challenging concept.

In the fluorescent-lit stainless-steel glare of the brew house, we schlep sacks of dusty malt, boxes of pelletized hops and sterile containers of yeast. Brewers don't usually get to walk through beautiful fields of living grain, witness the stunning hyper-growth of hop bines, or actually see what yeast looks like and how it behaves. We wouldn't consider plants as living organisms because they're just ingredients in a recipe, stuff that we eat, industrial commodities.

I was never a tree-hugger, more a tree-cutter, splitter and burner. I never thought about plants at all, save for making a salad and avoiding poison ivy. Then I married an herbalist. After living with April O'Keefe for fifteen or so years, plants are now a huge part of my life. Over time, being around her and essentially living in her apothecary got me to appreciate our green allies and how crucial they are to our survival. Here's her guiding mantra:

GREAT SPIRIT, MOTHER OF EVERYTHING,
BLESS OUR GREEN COMPANIONS.
EVER PATIENT, THEY MANIFEST ON EARTH
THE DEPTH AND BREADTH OF YOUR UNCONDITIONAL LOVE.

Wild carrot flowers, also known as Queen Ann's Lace

I had no clue what she was talking about, and I had no reason to consider it. Now, since I've become a brewer, I get goosebumps when I read it. Plants are our food, or at least food for our food, and our medicine and for some of us, our livelihood. They alone are responsible for producing that certain chemical that we cannot survive without: oxygen. That, my friend, is a very big deal.

A big reason why most people don't "get" plants is that people move fast and plants move very slowly. Speed up some video of plants, whether above ground or under the ground, and it becomes clear they're doing the same things the rest of us living organisms are: searching for nourishment, avoiding danger, communicating with each other and adapting to/dealing with whatever the world throws our way. Susun Weed, one of the preeminent herbalists in the United States, explains:

> *Herbs can change their constituents dramatically in response to being grazed, overgrazed, attacked by insects or molds, experiencing drought or flood, suffering from lack of nutrients, poisoned by too much, or a host of other variables.*

Plants are actually aware; they can sense what is happening to themselves and what is going on around them. Not only are they aware, they are also responsive. They alter their chemistry when a stressor presents itself, to survive and reproduce just as any other "higher" organism does. That includes communication, both to other plants and to other organisms.

FUNGUS AMONG US

In the November 2007 issue of *Scientific American*, Melinda Wenner wrote an article titled "Humans Carry More Bacterial Cells than Human Ones," subtitled "You are more bacteria than you are you." Whaaaat?! Growing up in a germ-phobic home in a germ-phobic society, this was a revelation. Like all animals, we humans are literally walking universes of microscopic life "from our skin to the deepest recesses of our guts." There is more non-human DNA in us than human DNA! Were you aware that in the average human, bacterial cells outnumber our own cells 10 to 1? What was even more shocking to me was learning that all these little buggers actually keep us alive. It's not just about all our internal organs doing their part; the reality is that they do their part in concert with most of those microbes. They aren't all just little invaders making us dirty or sick. Many of them are our indispensable partners in continued life!

Found moose skull, decorated and hung　　　　　*The mythical turkey shaman*

So yeast, a fungus, along with certain bacteria, are also our partners in brewing. Without these living entities, beer would not exist, nor would wine, spirits, yogurt, etc. Unlike hops, herbs or water, yeast feeds and reproduces and expels waste. It is alive like you, like me, like your brew-buddy Steve. If your yeast is not happy and healthy you will not be able to make good beer, period. And of course yeast isn't one entity—it is billions, trillions of individual yeast cells living out their lives. When that pitch of #1540 yeast hits your 65°F (19°C) fresh wort, its inhabitants enter a reproductive frenzy that will last for days, weeks or maybe years on end depending on how many waves of yeast and bacterial activity are sought—*if* they've been well cared for.

Think of it this way: You've spent hours preparing this awesome feast of sugar water. When the food is at its ideal temperature, the special guests arrive, via smack pack or a sanke keg or they've taken the tube from across the brewery. After the guests are seated and the sweet meal is deemed acceptable, the feasting begins. Not only are the guests gorging on the fine food, they are, ahem, reproducing right there on the dining room table. More importantly, they're also relieving themselves as well, the whole point of the party. The jacked-up guests are wantonly burping volumes of CO_2 and, sorry, peeing copious amounts of alcohol. After days of gluttony, the guests eventually fall asleep and if the food was very rich, most of them will die, poisoned in their own waste. It always makes me uncomfortable to ponder this, but it seems an important acknowledgment: Essentially, alcohol is yeast urine.

ALTERED STATUS

That bacchanalian scene leads me to ponder what is arguably the end game of brewing. I enjoy the tickle of a few beers on a fairly regular basis. Add a few thirsty people to the room and inevitably communication will ensue. Beer as social lubricant is perhaps its most often touted blessing, and I have received this blessing countless times. Something about that aforementioned tickle opens folks up a bit, provides some common ground and relaxes that self-doubt that many of us carry around, at least in moderation. In excess? I think we all know where that road goes.

Alcohol has fueled many important advances throughout time, not the least of which was the American Revolution. It was in taverns over tankards of ale that our forefathers first hatched the idea of independence from England. Gripes were aired, ideas were debated, solutions were developed, outcomes were explored and a country was born, all punctuated by, "Another ale, good sir?"

But people were getting intoxicated long before any countries existed. Virtually every group of people in every corner of the world had a means to altered states, whether it was smoked, eaten or drunk. Many of the herbs mentioned in this book are quite potent in this regard, however in much greater quantity than one would want to use in a beer. To be sure, we are after different flavors here, as in smell and taste rather than flavors of consciousness or perception. That being said, it is probable that one benefits in some subtle way, physiologically and/or psychologically, from a gruit "micro-dosing."

Anthropologists believe humans learned such imbibing behavior from observing animals and insects. Perhaps the most amazing observation is that plants also seek altered states! In his book, *Plant Intelligence and the Imaginal Realm*, Stephen Buhner explores sensory gating, a process that generally serves to protect us from the flood of sensory information we are bombarded with by limiting what we become conscious of. Certain fungi, and the product of certain fungi—that is, alcohol—can relax that gating—in other words, expand our consciousness by allowing more sensory information in.

> *When the doors of perception open more widely, the organism can more readily perceive the metaphysical background of the world, more deeply experience the underlying patterns that are at work, perceive a greater range of the meanings that are encoded in sensory data streams and begin to generate responses outside of habituated parameters. (p. 191)*

Just as the chemical "gift" given from a fungus to a plant can stimulate new root growth patterning in response to a stressor in the plant's habitat, a similar gift from fungus to humans can also stimulate new socio-political growth patterning in response to a stressor in the human's habitat, such as how the North American colonialists dealt with the British in the late 1700s. In his book, *Uncorking the Past*, archaeologist and anthropologist Patrick E. McGovern puts it another way:

> *The needs of homo sapiens include social rituals that bring the community together, artwork that symbolizes the workings of the mind and nature and religious rituals that give human experience meaning and coherence. A fermented beverage or drug can enhance these experiences and stimulate innovative thought. (p. 22)*

Toward the end of his book, the frequent Dogfish Head brewery collaborator offers:

> *From a very positive perspective, a mind-altering fermented beverage holds out the promise of individual and cultural renewal by encouraging and nourishing creativity and innovation of unusually imaginative individuals—"shamanistic spirits"—who are able to transcend traditions and think outside the box. (p. 278)*

ARE YOU LISTENING?

There is another level of plant communication that ties into the primitive mind. It involves the age-old practice of "listening" to plants, not with your ears necessarily, but with your awareness. It's not a big deal, it's just about being open to what calls to you. You might be doing yard work or out for a hike, and suddenly a particular plant gets your attention. You may even dream of a particular plant—don't dismiss it. Keep in mind that like a plant, we humans are of the earth too. We all come from the same cosmic slop so it shouldn't be too hard to consider a bit of interspecies communication. Various cultures around the world have been doing it for millennia, with some even considering this a magical act.

Once a plant has gotten your attention, snap a picture of it and take some notes on what it smells like along with any other interesting attributes you notice, but don't taste it unless you know what it is. Do some research, talk to your local experts, identify it and find out if it's ingestible or not. Proper plant identification is not just a good idea, it is a serious responsibility. Familiarize yourself with basic plant anatomy because accurate identification is about observing details. Keep in mind that "look alikes" pervade the plant kingdom. The difference between an eatable and a poison is sometimes very slight.

Get to know your local experts, the herbalists, farmers and foragers, and if there is a university nearby, reach out to some of its personnel. Chances are there is a professor or grad student in the botany department who would delight in helping you safely identify plants for your beer, particularly in exchange for said beer. Whether you're purchasing your botanicals on the Internet, buying them from a farmer or herbalist, or growing or foraging your own, always know what you're working with. When you've done your homework and you feel confident working with a particular plant, it's time to brew.

PRE-BREW

THE WILD CRAFT

If you want to forage for your plants (also called wildcrafting) be careful of where and how you harvest. Even though a plant might have caught your attention growing alongside the road, in a drainage ditch or an abandoned lot, avoid harvesting from such places. If there is even a slight chance that these plants have been exposed to chemicals, waste or pollution, stay away—as they will, of course, also contain whatever was in that soil. Chances are if you widen your search, you can find your plant in an area that's relatively clean.

Another concern when foraging is sustainability. An easy way to think of this is in terms of sharing—those plants are not just for you and your brew. Animals may need to eat it, certainly some type of bug is making its home in it and someone else may need some too. Never take more than a quarter of any one stand of plants—harvesting less is better (unless it's an invasive like Japanese knotweed or Scotch broom—plenty of that around!). It would be great if there was still some of the plant standing to reproduce and ensure its survival.

There are also endangered and protected plants out there—these are strictly hands off. Plants do go extinct, just like animals. Unfortunately, some have already become rare thanks to mankind's activities, whether through climate change, bulldozing habitat for the next strip mall or simply over-harvesting. A forager needs to be thinking on a level beyond their personal needs, always remaining conscious of all the other stressors on the plant and honoring its place in the forest/field/swamp. If you take it all, there will be nothing to come back to. Cooperate, don't obliterate!

COLLATERAL DAMAGE

I had just received a delivery of beautiful vibrant sweet fern from our forager, Jenna. After I had stripped the leaves off of a quarter of the plants to prep them for brewing, I realized that not only were they crawling with tiny bugs, I was too. The bowl I was putting the leaves in was like a bug circus, an insect on every single leaf it seemed. Part of Jenna's routine is to de-bug her wares before delivery, typically by shaking and rinsing them. These little guys were apparently too small to be effectively removed with a rinse and a shake.

The amazingly flavorful and common sweet fern

Ahimsa means, "do no harm." It's a major tenet in some Eastern religions and it's something I try and practice regularly . . . except with insects out to do me harm! It was disturbing to be faced with the prospect of killing a lot more of these bugs in order to prep this sweet fern. I carefully brushed off the bugs that were crawling on me, at least the ones I could see. I then very forcefully shook each stalk in our yard, one by one, watching the bugs slowly float through the air onto the weeds below. Rather than boil all those bugs alive in my wort, I dumped the bowl in the backyard, leaves and all. Karmic load lightened!

So if you are using foraged or wildcrafted herbs, remember that these plants are habitat for all sorts of little critters, critters who are doomed if they wind up on your brewery floor or in your wort. Be sure to do your due diligence, and make sure your forager does too. And if some do get through and wind up in your brew? No worries, a little extra protein won't hurt it, promise. That, of course, brings up the whole weird world of brewing with insects—on purpose—but that will have to wait.

MR. AND MRS. CLEAN

If you are an experienced brewer, you know you are actually a janitor who gets to brew 10 percent of the time. You have a full understanding and appreciation of the terms "clean" and "sanitized." Clean as in breaking down, cleaning, inspecting and perhaps re-cleaning everything you brew with thoroughly on a regular and routine basis, each time you brew. You know that anything that doesn't get cleaned will add some amount of off-flavor, something no self-respecting brewer would accept. Sure, constant cleaning is a pain in the ass, but it's time well spent—we all know it's the best insurance for good-tasting brew.

Sanitizing is not merely a ten-minute cycle with Star San or peracetic acid, right? It's really about the brewer thinking like bacteria. Remember the big feast metaphor? Your carefully prepared dinner of chilled wort is a dream come true for the billions of microbes floating in the air of your brewery. Unless you're Jean Van Roy at Cantillon Brewery in Belgium and you depend on house-microbes to ferment your beer, you'll want to exercise complete control over what gets to dine on that wort. All those brew surfaces need to be disinfected as well. That means keeping systems closed after that sani cycle, making sure you are not providing access to anything on the cool side of your brewing regimen.

Gruit wort is a different dish than its hopped cousin. Without the same level of antibacterial protection that hops provide, gruit wort is especially vulnerable, even though many of the useable herbs out there are allegedly antibacterial also. It seems as though a vat of warm sugar water can be too much for most gruit herbs to really protect—don't forget that!

CONTROL ISSUES

And, just to throw a curve ball into this whole issue, you might have the perfect cleaning/sanitizing routine and still wind up with an unplanned sour gruit on occasion. This had been the most vexing part of brewing them, at least in our experience. Typically, an infected beer is an obviously bad thing, and there's no doubt when it tastes like paint thinner. But what about when something uninvited, but not necessarily bad, shows up?

About a quarter or so of our gruits have come out as spontaneous unplanned sours and, because they were unplanned, we dumped the first couple batches and kept revisiting and adjusting our cleaning/sanitizing routines. The souring rate remains the same. In desperation, we brought some of this beer around to our more experienced brewing neighbors and, to our surprise, we were told "Hey, nice sour!" and "Don't dump that, folks will love it!" Our pals at Smuttynose Brewery in New Hampshire even ran some lab tests on it—no bad bugs were found. As we had more and more people taste it and continued to hear positive feedback, we were gradually able to let go of our expectations and embrace these beers—no easy chore!

Know your sugar content *From bucket to bag*

It seems that "off-flavors" are often more about what a particular style of beer shouldn't taste like, rather than being about bad flavors per se. Some flavors, such as estery, grassy, vegetal, alcoholic, medicinal, sour and oxidized, are a few that can actually work in some, but definitely not many, beers. In excess, these are all unacceptable flavors. There is another level of off-flavors that are simply not enjoyable in any amount, period. For example, Band-aidy, soapy, sulfuric, metallic or solvent-like flavors in the slightest amount signal a clear and obvious fail. Make no mistake: A bad beer is a bad beer! It's always a heart breaker but if you have to dump the beer, *dump the beer!* The only way to make a failed beer a success is to dump, review, adjust and re-brew. Discard that nasty stuff, review the thorough notes you always take and adjust where needed. Review your brewing and cleaning processes and adjust where needed, and then try brewing it again!

I fully expect that some of you are having a rough time with the idea of accepting, let alone releasing, a beer that did not come out the way it was planned. Wound up with something unexpected? Put your expectations aside for a minute and consider the beer on its own merits. Put together a taste panel to get some other opinions. Great beer is not always (gulp!) a product of meticulous planning and execution.

During the course of writing this book, we made a significant discovery—something that was staring us in the face all along. When we began home brewing, we used liquid yeast assuming that the active stuff would give us a better beer than the dried version. Liquid yeast is also quite a bit more expensive, so like many breweries we began to re-use pitches to save money. This worked fine with our traditional hopped beers, but eventually we began to notice that gruits behaved differently.

We realized that those fermented with a fresh pitch never went spontaneously sour. After the first generation, all bets were off, as re-pitching yielded more and more spontaneous sours with each successive use. We are not exactly sure what happens with the sours, but our assumption is that particular herbs and/or herb blends stress the yeast more than others, probably by dropping pH levels. As a result, later generations become progressively weaker and perhaps lose their ability to compete with the rich flora and fauna that inhabit the air in our tiny brewery. Maybe when we have a few extra grand laying around we can get the white coats in to verify our little theory. In the meantime, we have begun to use fresh pitches of cheaper and equally as effective dry yeast, which we discard after one use—unless of course we want a sour beer, in which case we will re-pitch and play the odds.

BAG ETIQUETTE

Plant fragments can really louse-up a brew day. Clogged kettle ports, re-circ tubing and/or wort chillers are just no way to fly. We also have a hop filter we can hook in between our boil kettle and wort chiller but that can get clogged too. We've got some large heavy-duty nylon bags, but they're only useful for high-volume wet-hopping. Our favorite method for introducing non-hop plant matter is the good ol' muslin bag. They work like a charm with leaf, flower, small sticks and most root material. Where they aren't helpful is when you're adding anything powdered, but we'll come back to that. Depending on what you're putting in there, you'll want to do some processing first. Cutting up leaves and flowers first will help. To get the most out of your plants, fill the bags

Like an oversized tea bag *Always take accurate measurements and detailed notes*

no more than two-thirds full so that when saturated, the material has room to expand. The more of it that has contact with the wort the better the flavor extraction will be. After you put your herb(s) into the bag, knot it as close to the opening as possible to allow maximum volume. Then rub the bag and its contents for a few seconds between your hands to bruise the material.

We made some S-shaped hooks with unpainted clothes hanger wire to hang bags in our kettle. Just cut a length and bend away. Hook one end through the top of the bag and the other on the rim of your kettle. The bag should be in full contact with the wort from the knot on down. If not, you'll need a longer hook or you can forgo hooks all together and use some fishing line. Tie one end to the bag and the other to a kettle handle or other outside anchor. Again, the line will need to be long enough so that the bag can fully submerge.

It's important to make sure the contents of your bags are fully saturated either by repeatedly dropping it in and pulling it out or holding it beneath the surface with a clean spoon or other utensil until the contents are completely wet. Some folks add weights to the bag so it immediately submerges—you'll just have to remember to take that weight out before you discard the bag. Regardless of the method, occasionally pull the bag out, let most of the liquid drain back into the kettle and then put the bag back. This helps to draw out more of the flavor into your wort, just like you'd do with a tea bag.

For much larger batches, we like what the crew at Cambridge Brewing Company has fabricated: a big stainless-steel mesh box, tethered by a chain. Looking like a well-used ancient brewing relic, or maybe some medieval torture device, a lid simply swings open, plant matter is dumped in, the lid clangs shut and is secured. The box is then lowered into the boil kettle at the appropriate time, the weight of the box more than compensating for the buoyancy of the plants.

OF POWDERS AND SYRUPS

Bashing up hard mushrooms and grinding dried berries is a novel pursuit when you first start doing it, but after a few times it becomes a time-consuming pain. Powdered forms of many herbs are readily available, and using them would be a win on two levels: an obvious time saver and a way to get more of the compounds out of the plant from the more thorough processing. Much like coffee, however, my experience is that nothing beats processing right before use. The pre-powdered stuff I experimented with just didn't seem as potent. Even though I feel very good about my suppliers, I wondered how old it was, how it was stored and what the quality of that plant matter really was.

Sometimes you're just stuck. There are other powdered or granular ingredients you'll want to add to your beer, such as certain sugars. Rather than adding such things straight to your boil kettle with a stir, hoping it dissolves before it settles to the bottom, try this: A few minutes before you need to make your addition, draw off some of your hot wort into a smaller metal cooking pot. Stir in your powdered herb, sugar, honey, molasses or sugar syrup with a whisk. Avoid introducing lots of air into the mix by stirring too fast. Take your time and make sure everything is completely dissolved/blended. Then slowly pour and stir the mixture back into your boil kettle.

A false bottom is a good friend   *Plant stripping, it's a thing*

A LITTLE BIT EXTRA

Referring to ancient Celtic and Druid practices, Stephen Buhner stated, "Many of the plants that were used, like yarrow, are innocuous or only mildly stimulating alone. When included in a fermenting beverage, however, their effects can increase dramatically." After putting this idea to the test multiple times with various herbs, our experience is inconclusive. If you decide to give this a try, keep these points in mind.

First, the herb(s) you add may interfere with or actually prevent fermentation. This happened to us once after adding cedar berries. The wort would not budge, even after multiple yeast pitches, and we had to finally dump it. Second, a potential contamination issue can occur with yeast/bacteria. If you're adding something that has not been frozen or heated, it will most likely have living microbes on it that will compete with the pitched yeast for sugars; this can potentially lead to an unexpected sour beer. To circumvent that issue, we added bags of herb to our fermenters that we had in hot wort for at least ten minutes. Finally, you do not want to do any tea-bagging or stick anything into your chilled, and thus vulnerable, wort. Either of these methods will introduce air and its microbial contents into the wort. Just use some kind of sanitized weight in the bag so you can open the vessel, drop the bag in and close it as quickly as possible. Oh, and tie it off too. You'll want to pull that bag out before you transfer the contents.

EXHILARATION

Exhilaration comes from the concept that beers without hops are stimulating in their effects, even aphrodisiacal, especially in this combination of herbs. This holy trinity of herbs is sweet gale, wild rosemary (not culinary rosemary) and yarrow. The first two are typically found in wetlands and swamps in northern climates with a strong winter season. Yarrow, on the other hand, grows just about everywhere. As you might imagine, the pre-Reformation version of a beer buzz was a much more animated, energetic and spirited affair than when hops came to rule.

Exhilaration is based on the herb combination that always seems to bubble up first when researching gruit. This combination points to origins in the British Isles, Scandinavia and the rest of Northern Europe. I first came across it in Stephen Buhner's *Sacred and Herbal Healing Beers*, an absolute must for anyone's beer and/or herbal library.

Not all are in agreement with the authenticity of these herbs being used together. "Sweet gale and marsh rosemary do not grow in the same areas (in Europe), hence making the combination unlikely and furthermore, since the two plants have similar flavors, and similar effects, why would you want to use them both?" asks beer historian Martyn Cornell, on his blog, Zythophile. In North America, sweet gale is far more prevalent than marsh rosemary, and often in areas where marsh rosemary does grow, one will find sweet gale nearby. I don't know why that wouldn't be the case in Europe. I would also beg to differ on the similarities point too. As one who has used both these herbs many times, both together and separately, they are aren't similar enough to preclude using one with the other.

Wild rosemary or marsh rosemary (*Rhododendron tomentosum*, formerly *Ledum palustre*) and a sub-species Labrador tea (*Rhododendron groenlandicum*, formerly *Ledum groenlandicum*), grow in the same conditions as sweet gale but are exclusive to more northern boreal areas. While these are two different plants, their close relationship elicits much confusion when doing research—their names often get used interchangeably. Both plants' active ingredients are concentrated in the flower tops but are in the foliage as well. They have a history of use as a first-aid remedy for puncture wounds and as an anti-parasitic, as well as treating back problems, insect stings, joint, muscle, arthritic, cough, cold and nerve pain. Recent research into the plants' essential oil preparation points to anti-oxidant, anti-diabetic and anti-cancer possibilities, according to PubMed (http://www.ncbi.nlm.nih.gov/pubmed/23352748). The Russian variety also has a history of ethnobotanical use by Siberian tribes.

Sweet gale (Myrica Gale) leaves

Wild rosemary's strong smell attracts pollinating insects

"Despite its toxicity it has been cleverly used to flavor beer, instead of or alongside hops. Essential oils stimulate the central nervous system, so drinkers can become sexually excited or quarrelsome troublemakers. This quickly passes however and is replaced by apathy," according to NatureGate. And then comes a rather sobering warning regarding "shocking hangovers" and kidney failure. Happy to report that after brewing many batches containing both wild rosemary and Labrador tea, no kidneys were destroyed and no shocking hangovers were experienced.

Yarrow (*Achillea millefolium*) is the third herbal ingredient. Its stem is sort of rough, with alternating fern-like feathery leaves. Its large, flat flower head is actually hundreds of tiny flowers that range from white to a faint pink. It grows literally everywhere and has been used by native peoples all over the world. Herbalist Matthew Wood refers to it as "one of the primal remedies of the Western herbal tradition" and "master of the blood."

Yarrow has been employed for multiple conditions and ailments for at least 60,000 years, as evidenced by the contents of a Neanderthal grave in Iraq. Achilles used yarrow to stop bleeding on the battlefield. We're talking serious wounds from flesh-piercing weapons like spears, swords, knives and arrows, the type that need to get stitched up!

Sweet gale catkins—tiny flavor grenades!

It also enjoys a long relationship with beer. The eighteenth-century botanist Linnaeus wrote of yarrow beer brewed in Sweden for weddings "so that the guests become crazy" because it "brings about special sensations and feelings." Not the least of these feelings was a heightened sense of arousal. For our purposes, using yarrow for taste rather than psychological properties, it imparts a pleasant bitter flavor and has many of the same preservative properties as hops.

Sweet gale or bog myrtle (*Myrica gale*) may be the quintessential gruit herb. This deciduous, perennial shrub grows around four feet (1.2 m) tall in wet soil at the edge of lakes, ponds and streams. It has narrow, oblanceolate leaves that taper at the base. The upper side of the leaf is a glossy dark green with a lighter underside. Sweet gale also produces extremely fragrant clusters of catkins, which are the tiny cone-looking fruits.

Buhner claimed that it's been used to make ale stronger throughout Europe for millennia. In Yorkshire, England, it was used as a substitute for hops and put into a thirst-quencher called "gale beer," according to Margaret Grieve in *A Modern Herbal*. She also states that in China, sweet gale leaves are used as a tea, producing a stomachic and cordial drink. It all sounds rather innocent until you start coming across references to the Berserkers, elite Norse warriors who were famous for fighting in a frenzied trance wearing animal skins instead of the standard-issue chain mail. Numerous sources point to a sweet gale–infused ale called "porsøl" or "por," which helped get the troops into this fearless frame of mind!

EXHILARATION

YIELD: 5 GALLONS (18.9 L), ALL-GRAIN

11 lb (5 kg) 92% 2-row pale malt (e.g., Maris Otter)

7 oz (200 g) 4% biscuit or victory malt

7 oz (200 g) 4% melanoiden malt

Total Grain Bill: 11.88 lb (5.4 kg)

Mash Water: 3.67 gallons (13.89 L)

Sparge Water: 3.44 gallons (13.02 L)

Mash Temperature: 151°F (66°C)

Sparge Water Temperature: 168°F (76°C)

Boil Time: 1 hour

HERBS, ETC.*

0.5 oz (14 g) ½ @ 15 minutes, ½ @ flame-out (f/o) sweet gale

0.5 oz (14 g) ½ @ 15 minutes, ½ @ flame-out (f/o) wild rosemary

0.5 oz (14 g) ½ @ 15 minutes, ½ @ flame-out (f/o) yarrow

YEAST

Wyeast Scottish 1728

Target OG: 1.064

Target FG: 1.014

ABV: 6.6%

Add the herbs at flame-out, keep immersed through ten-plus-minute whirlpool and ten-plus-minute settle, for at least twenty minutes of total contact time.

These same herbs can then be added to a fermenter to further enhance flavor. If you decide to do this, make sure all areas of the herb bags have been sterilized by contact with hot wort. Also, put a sterilized weight, like a tri-clamp, in the bag to ensure maximum contact with the wort. Don't forget to take it out when you toss the bag!

After you have brewed this and feel like you have a sense of the basic beer, do tweak this recipe! Grain-wise, any 2-row is fair game, particularly local grain or at least grain from a local maltster. You might want to add a bit of smoked grain or a more authentic rendition. It's thought that medieval beer had at least a touch of smoke in its flavor, as malt was kilned and wort was boiled over wood fires. Some wheat or rye malt could take Exhilaration into some tasty places too!

Herb-wise, there's infinite room for experimentation. Juniper could be a great addition. Toss some fresh branches into your hot liquor tank (HLT) while you get your water up to temp and/or add some as your wort boils. If you have juniper berries, break them up in a coffee grinder, bag them and toss them in at fifteen minutes.

Note: Amounts are for dried herb. If fresh, double the amounts. Cut up the leaf and flowers, place in a muslin bag, and bruise herb by squeezing and rubbing the bag vigorously. Sweet gale twigs can also be broken up and used also.

TASTING NOTES

Brewer's Note: *Pours a light brown. Moss, loam and whole grain bread on the nose, with citrus and celery notes. Creamy yet crisp, sweet savory spice to bready citrus notes then working into the sourdough bread and yeast slight notes of citrus. Light tartness. Crisp and smooth, complex and interesting on the tongue.*

ONLINE BEER REVIEWS

BeerAdvocate.com Members:

"The beer pours a beautiful light candied brown, bordering on orange and amber, with a great tightly packed white head that fizzles down to about a quarter of a finger's width scrim. The body of the beer is a murky haze, but it does seem to be mildly translucent. On the nose this beer smells terrifically earthy. The rosemary can also be felt strongly in the background of the smell, producing a feel that is much akin to how mint hits the nose. This beer tastes fantastic."

BLOOMERS

A flower is the reproductive part of a floral plant. The transfer of pollen is what causes fertilization. The wonderful colors and fragrances flowers emit are all in the service of pollen transfer. Animals and insects are attracted and either purposefully gather or otherwise collect pollen, some of which is shed on the next flower they visit. Once this pollen has been received and a flower has become fertilized, the ovary grows into a fruit in which seeds are found. Humans have not been immune to their charms. Not only do we give our loved ones flowers on special occasions, but we have used them ritually, medicinally and nutritionally for millennia. So it's natural to use them in beer.

Any edible flower is potentially fair game for brewing. The real work of it is to identify the smell and flavor of each and capture enough of that essence to have it present in a beer. We brew Bloomers in late spring/early summer to showcase the season's bounty. There are waves of flowers blooming everywhere throughout the spring and summer, a phenomenon that expresses a place and a time like nothing else. We tend to let nature guide our flower choices, finding that most flowers that bloom at the same time in the same area do very well together in the same beer. Different versions could be brewed repeatedly throughout the summer months as different groups of plants flower. There is much variation in the strength of this dizzying array of scents and flavors. For that reason, the grain bill is a very light one, both color-wise and flavor-wise. The intent is to provide a neutral canvas for the floral notes to shine on, with a bit of subtle yet complementary malt flavors.

Black elder (*Sambucus nigra*) grows in temperate to subtropical regions in Europe and North America. It typically grows as larger shrubs and occasionally small trees. It is fairly easy to identify in early summer with its characteristic flat-topped clusters of small white flowers—the parts we are after for this recipe. Later in the summer the flowers transform into drooping clusters of bluish to jet-black berries, a harbinger of summer's end and great ingredients for beer as well. However, if the berries are red, stay away! Another elder variety, *Sambucus racemosa*, is poisonous.

Elder was once known as the elder mother or queen of the underworld, and the bush itself was a portal through which to enter her world of faeries and sprites, according to herbalist Matthew Wood. As a result, one should never have slept under an elder tree and cradles were never made of its wood. The name elder comes from *hulda*, which means hidden, rather than the oft-cited *eld*, which means fire. Huldafolk, also known as faeries, were thought of as occupying the underworld. Sambucus comes from the sambuka, a musical instrument made from the hollow stems of the elder, also called a pan pipe or pan flute. The pan flute refers to Pan, the Lord of the Underworld. Cultures as diverse as North American Indians and European peasants made offerings to the plant and even asked it for permission before using its wood. The lore of this powerful plant continues on and on, from country to country, and age to age.

The elder is viewed in all ancient texts as a panacea, a cure-all—pan-acea, as in Pan's sacred healing power of the forest coming through "his most sacred plant." Each part of the plant has specific healing properties. The flowers, regularly eaten in many countries, provide a stimulative effect when prepared in a warm solution. They also help to remove excess mucous from the body, fighting ear, sinus and throat infections. "Folk legend has it that continued use of elder will heal all the ills a person is likely to have in their lifetime, thus promoting long life and giving rise to its name, elder," according to Stephen Buhner.

Sage (*Salvia officinalis*) enjoys a long history in brewing and a much longer one in herbalism. While there are many varieties, look for the one that's native to your area. Fortunately, they can all be used interchangeably. The botanical name *salvia* originates from the Latin *salvus* meaning "to make healthy." "Sage has long had a reputation as an herb that mitigates mental and bodily grief, heals the nerves, counter-acts fear and protects human beings from evil influences, spiritual and physical," according to Buhner. While its leaves get most of the attention, we are interested in its blooms for this recipe. Purple and/or white flowers appear on sage plants in the early summer. The ones that grow in northern New England have a unique sweet/peppery flavor that is a slam-dunk for beer. Pluck a flower off the stalk, pop it in your mouth and I'm sure you'll agree. The tough part of using these flowers is that the window for collecting them is pretty narrow, maybe two weeks if you're lucky. The ideal harvest time is when the flowers are just starting to open, once the morning dew has evaporated. As usual, be sure you know what you're harvesting and, if possible, confirm that the area it's growing in has not been sprayed with insecticide.

Perhaps you are familiar with the ubiquitous dandelion plant (*Taraxacum officinale*)? Cursed weed, bane of every lawn owner? Hopefully you will never look at this mighty plant the same way. Its name comes from the shape of its leaves, according to M. Grieve. The leaves were thought to resemble the teeth of a lion, *dent de lion* in French or *dens leonis* in Latin. She further states that because of its "lavishly supplied nectar . . . no less than 93 different kinds of insects are in the habit of visiting it." Birds love the seeds, pigs the whole plant and humans have been eating all parts for nourishment and medicine for centuries. It is good for the liver, kidneys and upper respiratory system, and its flowers can have a calming effect when taken in tea. That's just for starters!

Wild carrot and meadowsweet flowers

The venerable locust tree

Someone figured out it was pretty good in beer, most likely as a way to administer its medicinal properties. Its roots are one of the ingredients in traditional root beer. "Dandelion beer is a rustic fermented drink common in many parts of the country (England) and made also in Canada," Grieve reported. The leaves and the roots are both viable additions, but here we are looking for those bright yellow flowers.

The most delicate flower is from North America's strongest timber tree, black locust (*Robinia pseudoacacia*). They originated in the Eastern United States, and they've been introduced throughout the world. They handle pollution well so they're planted in cities, they grow fast and thus control erosion well, and they contribute to an area's honey supply. Black locust is also regarded as an invasive species in many places for the same reasons. It has a long history, particularly as a rot-resisting building material in revolution-era United States. "It has the highest beam strength of any North American tree, and . . . a cord of seasoned locust has the same Btu potential as a ton of anthracite coal—the highest fuel value of any American tree," according to Wesley Greene, of the Colonial Williamsburg Foundation.

Some of the uses of black locust include stopping spasms, defense against viral attacks, purifying and energizing the body and as a cancer treatment, according to herbs2000.com. Reportedly a "heady" narcotic brew can be made from its seed pods, and the flowers have diuretic, emollient, laxative and purgative properties. But once again, we're brewing for taste rather than medicinal properties. You'll need to use far greater amounts of the correct plant part for any obvious health benefits.

Finally, there's wormwood (*Artemisia absinthium*), which originated in Europe, Africa and Asia. It now grows wild throughout much of the United States, often along paths, roadsides and other disturbed spaces. Typically, the leaves are used but the flowers are certainly fair game. Buhner reported wormwood is named for its ability to rid the digestive system of worms and other parasites. "The name wormwood comes from Old English/Old Saxon *wermod*, meaning something like 'defend the mind,'" according to Dale Pendell in his epic *Pharmako* trilogy. It's the same herb used in the often misunderstood, highly alcoholic drink called absinthe and its use and reverence goes back to ancient times.

Many sources cite wormwood as an aphrodisiac as well as a nervine and digestive tonic, as well as a plethora of other medicinal and spiritual uses around the world in all sorts of varied cultures. "Comments about headiness and strength coming from its addition indicate that it does increase beer potency," according to Buhner. He goes on to state, "Wormwood is a member of the same family that contains chamomile, tansy and yarrow—all herbs reputed to possess mild narcotic properties and to increase inebriation when used as an adjunct in brewing." It is a spectacularly bitter herb which, like horehound, will destroy a beer if used too liberally. Used sparingly, it lends just the right amount of spicy bitterness to offset sweet malt and strong floral notes.

Much-tainted hay has been made from thujone, one of wormwood's chemical constituents. Not a hallucinogen but a potent convulsant, thujone was the reason absinthe was illegal for so long in most of the Western world. As it turns out, a person would have to consume upwards of forty bottles of absinthe before there was enough thujone in their system to do any actual harm. Clearly any mortal would be long dead from alcohol poisoning after a bottle or two! Banned in the United States in 1912, the authorities eventually relented for this reason and absinthe was once again legal in 2007.

There are reportedly more than 180 different species of *Artemisia* and many of them are fine for use in brewing; however, *A. absinthium* in particular is a must for genuine absinthe. Roman wormwood (*A. pontica*) is more aromatic and less bitter than its stronger cousin and is used in vermouth. We'll get to mugwort (*A. vulgaris*) later on, but sagebrush (*A. tridentata*) is a very compelling western U.S. native and tarragon (*A. dracunculus*) is, of course, a wonderful culinary herb. There is probably a species common to your location—do explore its brewing potential.

BLOOMERS

YIELD: 5 GALLONS (18.9 L), ALL-GRAIN

2 lb (0.9 kg) 24% 6-row pale malt

2 lb (0.9 kg) 24% 2-row pilsner malt

2 lb (0.9 kg) 24% Vienna malt

2 lb (0.9 kg) 24% white wheat malt

3.7 oz (105 g) 3% acidulated malt

Total Grain Bill: 8.2 lb (3.7 kg)

Mash Water: 2.57 gallons (9.73 L)

Sparge Water: 4.91 gallons (18.59 L)

Mash Temperature: 151°F (66°C)

Sparge Water Temperature: 168°F (76°C)

Boil Time: 1 hour

HERBS, ETC.

0.25 oz (7 g) @ 10 minutes dried wormwood

1 oz (28 g) @ flame-out (f/o) fresh elder flowers

1 oz (28 g) @ flame-out (f/o) fresh dandelion flowers

1 oz (28 g) @ flame-out (f/o) fresh sage flowers

1 oz (28 g) @ flame-out (f/o) fresh black locust flowers

YEAST

Wyeast Belgian Wheat #3942

Target OG: 1.039

Target FG: 1.007

ABV: 4.2%

Add the wormwood at ten minutes remaining to balance the malt's sweetness. If fresh, use 0.5 ounces (14 g), cut up stems and leaf, bag and bruise before adding. Also, 0.20 ounces (6 g) of horehound could do this job. Add the bagged and bruised flowers at flame-out. Keep immersed through ten-plus-minute whirlpool and ten-plus-minute settle for at least twenty minutes of total contact time.

More flowers can be added after the initial fermentation is complete, plus or minus four days, to further enhance flavor. Keep in mind that immediately freezing is the only way to store flowers if you can't use them within a day or two of harvesting. This will also kill off any yeast or bacteria on them. Freezing also breaks down cell walls, which can improve flavor yield. After a couple weeks in the freezer, however, flavors will start to wane. If there are still fresh flowers available, you could take a gamble on what microbes are living on the flowers. Any effects should be minimal since your beer is already mostly fermented. Having the bags float on the surface won't have much of an effect so if you decide to do this, put a sterilized weight, like a tri-clamp, in the bag to ensure maximum contact with the wort. Don't forget to take it out when you toss or compost the bag!

After you have brewed this and feel like you have a sense of the basic beer, do tweak this recipe. Other friendly flowers include yarrow, chamomile and nasturtium—any edible bloom is worth considering.

TASTING NOTES

Brewer's Note: *Cloudy gold with thin head. Earthy, spicy fruit, moss and medicinal berries. Grassy, floral notes linger. Toasted grain body on the light side of medium. As it warms up the elderflower comes out. Floral, dry finish. Yeast character balances the floral quality. Light mouthfeel, effervescent. Low herb bitterness.*

ONLINE BEER REVIEWS

Untappd.com Members

"Fresh tasting and with forged flowers? Amazing."

"Definitely getting the elderflowers in this one. And that's a good thing!"

"Tastes like a flower!"

"Not what I expected, definitely grew on me. As it warms up the elderflower comes out."

"I have absolutely nothing to compare this to. But I kind of like it, though it doesn't seem like 'beer'."

"Need a full pour. This is special."

"Very floral, nice dry finish."

"Really digging this flower bomb. Yeast character is pronounced and helps balance the floral quality."

"Locust flowers are quite interesting!!!"

"Getting lots of yarrow, aroma and taste, with a tang from the elderflowers; definitely a summer sipping gruit."

"Wow, one of the best beers I've had in a while."

"Nose of flowers, moss, medical berries. And herbs. Light mouthfeel, effervescent. Low herb bitterness."

"Perfect for a hot day. Not too fruity not too floral."

CHAGA GROOVE

There are lots of interesting ingredients waiting in the forests. Seasonality is the key and if it's early spring in New England, warm days and cold nights mean the maple sap will be running. My friend Daryl has been tapping the trees in his Southern Maine neighborhood for years. The bottle label we used for this beer features a few of those same trees and the rustic equipment Daryl employs. You'll also be using a rather ugly fungus that grows on birch trees called chaga. Do try and find some for yourself as it is pretty unmistakable, expensive to buy and a great excuse for a walk in the woods. You'll need some yarrow (page 38), and another ingredient, which you might find from the Spice Islands of Indonesia—nutmeg.

Sugar maple or rock maple (*Acer saccharum*) provides the brewing liquid for this beer. Other maples such as red or black are fair game as well. Native Americans discovered that by making small cuts and holes in a maple's trunk during this time, sap would exit the tree, which they could collect and boil, creating a very tasty sugar—perfect for beer! Starch accumulates in the roots and trunks, which changes into sugar in early spring to fuel the tree's new growth. There is a narrow window of time during which that sugar, along with water and nutrients, are pumped up the tree in the form of sap to its shoots and leaves. Prime tapping time occurs when nights are in the 20°F (-6.7°C) range and the days about 40°F (4.4°C), fluctuations that act as a thermal pump.

If you want to collect your own sap, it's a pretty simple process and there are plenty of resources out there to guide you. Keep in mind that this sap, like any solution with sugar in it, can and will ferment. Refrigerate your strained sap as soon as possible in a sanitized lidded container. You'll have a week or so before it gets funky—that's when the clear sap has become milky. If this happens, you don't necessarily have to dump it, just know that you will wind up with some very different flavors. We actually brewed a batch of a different beer with the last of the season's sap, some of which had been left out in buckets for weeks. It all smelled a bit musty and looked like milk, but we had to give it a try. Acer X turned out to be a unique and very drinkable sour.

Keep your barrels labeled

Semi-processed chaga mushroom

If you can't find sap, water with maple syrup added is certainly fine. Just make sure that it's authentic maple syrup and not the common maple-flavored corn sugar variety. You could also wait out the maple season to when the birch sap runs. Its sugars are twice as diluted as maple, so you might consider boiling some of the water off first.

Consider the tree, the longest-living organism on our planet. Think about the powerful nutrients that make such a long life possible, for some trees hundreds, even thousands of years. Now imagine a life form that not only absorbs these same nutrients but collects and concentrates them. This is why chaga (*Inonotus obliquus*) is called the "gift from God" and the "mushroom of immortality" by the Siberians, "the diamond of the forest" by the Japanese and the "king of plants" by the Chinese, according to Chagaknowledge.com.

It bears no resemblance whatsoever to a common mushroom, though. Instead, chaga grows into large protruding masses resembling charred wood on dead and dying birch trees. Rather than being soft and spongy, chaga is hard and wood-like, a rust-colored brown on the inside. It's been used medicinally in Russia and Asia for centuries, and it's becoming hugely popular now in the West. Some credible studies suggest it supports the immune system, helps in the fight against cancer and supports healthy cholesterol and blood pressure levels. Chaga is also an anti-inflammatory and an adaptogen, rich in anti-oxidants, beta-glucans and a host of other helpful compounds.

I have to admit, however, that it's with mixed feelings I suggest using this favorite of the Siberian shaman. As it becomes more and more popular, folks are harvesting it with abandon rather than responsibility. It takes a relatively long time for a big hunk of it to grow, three to ten years. Because its growth cycle is so much slower than seasonally occurring plants, it should be regarded with some reverence. Sustainable practices for a slow-growth plant are even more vital to its survival. Some foragers have even opted to no longer harvest it to ensure it does not become endangered.

The history of the spice trade is a lot more dramatic and bloody than you might know, particularly where the fruit of the *Myristica frangans* tree, nutmeg, is concerned. Perhaps best known in America for its holiday use as a spice in eggnog, nutmeg is also an aphrodisiac, stimulant and in large enough doses, a narcotic. Nutmeg is the seed, and mace is the dried fruit covering it. Wars were waged, genocide was perpetrated and the island of Manhattan passed from Dutch to English control because of its coveted qualities. Not very backwoodish, right? Well, remember that centuries ago, when the tree only grew on a clump of islands in the Pacific, some curious native discovered it in his or her backwoods. It's nothing short of amazing, and also tragic, to see the effect that discovery had on the known world.

Nutmeg is readily available in the spice aisle of your local grocery store. Whether it's actually good, as in properly prepared and taken care of, or whether it's actually nutmeg at all, is another story. There's a long history of old and ill-processed stuff being sold, even outright fakes. Connecticut is known as the nutmeg state not because it grows there, but because some of the state's spice merchants were famous for whittling little look-alike seeds out of wood and selling them as nutmeg. Although this ingredient isn't the most important in this recipe, do make some effort to procure the real deal—you'll be glad you did. Its nutty, slightly sweet, slightly bitter taste is a great complement to chaga and often shows up in various chaga products, particularly teas.

CHAGA GROOVE

YIELD: 5 GALLONS (18.9 L), ALL-GRAIN

9 lb (4 kg) 58% 2-row pale

3.5 lb (1.6 kg) 22% munich

1.5 lb (680 g) 10% amber

13 oz (369 g) 5% beechwood smoked

8 oz (227 g) 3% special b

4 oz (113 g) 1.6% chocolate

1 oz (28 g) 0.4% carafa 1

Total Grain Bill: 15.6 lb (7 kg)

Mash Water: 4.9 gallons (18.55 L) maple sap (or water)

Sparge Water: 3.5 gallons (13.25 L) maple sap (or water)

Mash Temperature: 151°F (66°C)

Sparge Water Temperature: 168°F (76°C)

Boil Time: 1 hour

HERBS, ETC.*

2.2 oz (62.4 g) ½ @ 20 minutes, ½ flame-out (f/o) chaga, processed

1 oz (28 g) ½ @ 10 minutes, ½ flame-out (f/o) yarrow, dried

0.2 oz (5.7 g) @ flame-out (f/o) nutmeg, ground

YEAST

Wyeast Scottish #1728

Target OG: 1.075

Target FG: 1.017

ABV: 7.6%

Break up the chaga into at least pea-sized pieces. I use a bash box to contain the flying pieces—just a clean cardboard box with the inside seams taped up. Use a chisel to split the chaga into 8 pieces and then a mallet to smash the pieces to size. Wear safety glasses and expect lots of dust during the process. Put half of the processed chaga in a bag and add to the boil at twenty minutes. Put half of the yarrow in a bag and add at ten minutes. Double the amount if fresh, cut up stems and leaf, bag and bruise before adding. Stir the nutmeg powder directly into the wort at flame-out. Also add the rest of the yarrow (double amount if fresh) and chaga, bagged. Keep immersed through ten-plus-minute whirlpool and ten-plus-minute settle for at least twenty minutes of total contact time.

While hot wort extracts some of the flavors/constituents, alcohol will extract others. Consider adding the last chaga/yarrow bag to your fermenter for the resulting alcohol. If you decide to do this, make sure all areas of the herb bags have been sterilized by contact with hot wort. Put a sterilized weight, like a tri-clamp, in the bag to ensure maximum contact with the wort. Don't forget to take it out when you toss the bag! You may even want to "dry hop" with a portion of the chaga, after fermentation is complete.

After you have brewed this and feel like you have a sense of the basic beer, do tweak this recipe! Consider switching out chaga for a different hard addition, like other polypore mushrooms or herb roots such as calamus. Yarrow could be substituted by

Note: Amounts are for dried herb. If fresh, double the amounts. Cut up the leaf and flowers, place in a muslin bag and bruise the herb by squeezing and rubbing the bag vigorously.

(continued)

any number of medium-strength herbs such as spikenard or sweet fern. Fenugreek can also boost the maple flavor of the finished beer, but too much will make it taste like celery. Two grams ought to do it. We were gifted with some real maple syrup recently, which will be added to this year's batch shortly before it is bottled/kegged. Of course the extra sugars from the syrup will need to ferment out first.

Chaga Groove ages quite well in oak barrels, we've used both bourbon and apple brandy barrels. We usually let it ride for between four and twelve months—well worth the wait!

TASTING NOTES

Brewer's Note: *Dark brown/black, with a decent head. Earthy, light root and herbal flavors, slight sweetness from maple. Spiciness and almost roasty flavor in aftertaste. Slight alcohol warming (along with some barreled booze and woody barrel notes) along with a bit of sour and bitterness in back of throat. Complex with many flavors.*

ONLINE BEER REVIEWS

BeerAdvocate.com Members

"Pours dark brown/black, earthy, root, herbal flavors, along with a lightness that almost reminded me of a sarsaparilla for some sips especially in the first batch. Slight sweetness from maple sap. Spiciness is noted as well, which must be from the nutmeg. An almost smoky flavor in aftertaste that gives it a lot of character."

MONKEY WEED

More commonly known as Japanese knotweed, monkey weed is a threat to native species from Maine to Oregon. Originally from East Asia, it is so voracious that it's actually illegal to grow or even possess it in some states and countries. It can penetrate concrete and asphalt, so roads, dams and buildings are all vulnerable to its power. It's also edible, rich in vitamin C and has medicinal properties, so it's no surprise we brew with it. We were honored to brew a batch with Zero Gravity Brewery of Vermont for the 2016 Vermont Brewer's Fest.

The catalyst for our recipe is an esoteric beer called Lichtenhainer, from the town of the same name in northern Germany—a sour beer with no souring bugs or yeasts added, just acidulated malt. We took that souring technique in a totally different direction that yielded a magical pink beer that's low in alcohol and high in refreshingly tart and curious flavors. If you're trying to conceive or are with child, avoid this one—two of the ingredients, spikenard and hibiscus, are not pregnancy-friendly.

Polygonum cuspidatum in North America, *Fallopia japonica* in Europe, *Itadori* or tiger staff in Japan and *Hu zhang* in China, Japanese knotweed features reddish-brown hollow stalks with lots of branches, spade-shaped leaves and particularly hardy and active rhizomes. A single plant can reach 4 to 8 feet (1.2 to 2.4 m) high and 65 feet (19.8 m) wide. It's almost frightening to consider that the smallest piece of knotweed will start an entirely new plant. Folks have learned the hard way that if you toss cuttings on your compost pile you will most assuredly have several knotweed plants taking it over. Always bag, burn or eat any cuttings—a unique precaution indeed.

There is a strong belief among many plant-connected people that invasive plants show up when and where they are needed. Turns out knotweed roots contain lots of resveratrol, which thins the blood and in turn fights cardiovascular disease. Resveratrol also inhibits tumor growth, enhances fat burning and straight-up kills Lyme bacteria. It has also been found effective in treating Alzheimer's disease and dementia.

As for its taste, Green Deane, of Eattheweeds.com fame, reported, "many folks say it tastes like rhubarb but I think a lemony green is more accurate, crunchy and tender." The tender shoots are a great substitute for rhubarb in a strawberry-rhubarb pie and crumble cake. "First, I just bit into it straight, and I fell in love with the taste," reported Ghaya Oliveira in her article in Bon Appetit. It's like rhubarb, but "more earthy. It tastes like rain." Knotweed is the "gamey" version of rhubarb, so she combines both in her desserts, letting the knotweed enhance the flavor of the rhubarb.

Harvest young shoots that are 12 inches (30 cm) tall or less in early spring. The taller the plants get, the greater the concentration of oxalic acid. This imparts a nice acidity in the small amounts that the shoots provide, but can be toxic from full-grown plants. Its tell-tale white flowers grow in large drooping bunches, and while it can grow almost anywhere the sun shines, it thrives along rivers and streams. It also likes roadsides and disturbed and/or waste areas—so be careful where you harvest it. If there's a chance the land has been treated with or contaminated by chemicals, keep looking! Because it's such a threat, folks bring out the big herbicide guns to kill it off, as simply cutting it back is no use.

I first came across spikenard (*Nardostachys jatamansi*) while reading the Bible. "Then took Mary a pound of ointment of spikenard, very costly and anointed the feet of Jesus, and wiped his feet with her hair: and the house was filled with the odor of the ointment."—John 12:3. There are plenty of references for its use in cooking and spicing-up wine and beer, including a wonderful English strong ale called Stingo. But this variety, which you might find if you were foraging in the Himalaya, is not the same spikenard you'll find in North America. It's American spikenard (*Aralia racemosa*) we're brewing with here.

Also known as wild or false sarsaparilla, *A. racemosa* was used by Native Americans and in American folk medicine for various ailments and as a cleansing spring tonic. This native species can be found throughout the northern half of the United States and Canada, usually in woodlands in the cracks and crevices of rock outcroppings. It flowers in July with star-burst-shaped arrays of tiny white or light green blooms. Later in the season, I'm told they yield some good-tasting berries that I would brew with in a heartbeat, but our forager hasn't bumped into any yet. It's the roots we're after here—spicy, licorice-like and uniquely aromatic, providing a good base note to this recipe.

The gloriously flowering hibiscus (*Hibiscus sabdariffa*) is native to West Africa—probably an ingredient you'll need to forage for at your neighborhood health food store or online. There are hundreds of hibiscus variations, but the ruby-red (*H. sabdaruffa*) flower and the Hawaiian hibiscus (*H. rosa-sinensis*) are often the go-tos for edible and drinkable applications. A red hibiscus flower is also recommended as an ingredient in love potions and is said to promote good fortune. It's rich in vitamin C and antioxidants, with antibacterial, anti-inflammatory and astringent properties—and that's just for starters. Hibiscus is consumed throughout tropical countries for it's tart, lemony and cranberry-like flavor, often as a tea.

MONKEY WEED

YIELD: 5 GALLONS (18.9 L), ALL-GRAIN

3.13 lb (1.4 kg) wheat malt

2.06 lb (940 g) pilsner

2.06 lb (940 g) flaked rice

1 lb (454 g) rice hulls

10.5 oz (298 g) acidulated malt

Total Grain Bill: 8.84 lb (4 kg)

Mash Water: 2.57 gallons (9.73 L)

Sparge Water: 4.91 gallons (18.57 L)

Mash Temperature: 151°F (66°C)

Sparge Water Temperature: 168°F (76°C)

Boil Time: 1 hour

HERBS, ETC.*

4.5 oz (128 g) @ ½ flame-out (f/o), ½ post-fermentation Japanese knotweed shoots

0.4 oz (11 g) @ ½ flame-out (f/o), ½ post-fermentation hibiscus

0.4 oz (11 g) @ ½ 10 minutes, ½ post-fermentation spikenard

YEAST

Wyeast Belgian #1214 or French Saison #3711

Target OG: 1.036

Target FG: 1.008

ABV: 3.7%

While you are mashing and/or boiling, purée half of your knotweed or cut it up as finely as possible, put in a muslin bag with half of the hibiscus and knot the bag as close to the opening as possible to allow maximum volume. Don't lose any of the juice. If you have fresh spikenard roots, chop up half of them as finely as possible, bag and knot. If you've bought it, it's probably dried and shredded.

Add the bagged spikenard to the boil at ten minutes and the knotweed/hibiscus bag at flame-out. Pour in any juice too. Keep immersed through ten-plus-minute whirlpool and ten-plus-minute settle for at least twenty minutes of total contact time.

Around four days before bottling or kegging, purée the rest of the knotweed, bag and add to fermenter along with any juice. Bag the remaining processed spikenard and hibiscus with a clean and sanitized weight in the bag and add to a fermenter.

It's fine to freeze the knotweed and pretty much anything else that's been foraged if there's going to be some time between harvest and brewing. While it kills off bacteria and opens cell walls, it's also just damn handy.

Note: Amounts are for dried herb. If fresh, double the amounts. Cut up the leaf and flowers, place in a muslin bag and bruise herb by squeezing and rubbing the bag vigorously.

TASTING NOTES

Brewer's Note: *Clear red with no head. Red grape, berry, a bit dry and floral on the nose. Some dry red wine, slight pepper, funky herbal tones. Bit tart with medium body and medium to high carbonation. Floral farmhouse meets fruit gose.*

ONLINE BEER REVIEWS

Untappd.com Members

"Not brewed with weed or monkeys. Still pretty good."

"Very interesting somewhat tart saison."

"Earthy and sweet flowers. Intrigued by the gruit."

"Very different. A very floral farmhouse."

"Almost tasted like a wine cooler."

"Great summer brew! Good balance!"

"Every time I get a saison, I forget they're not my favorite, but this one's a little sour and pretty yummy."

"Very nice gose type flavor with slight pepper taste."

"Really nice gruit, funky herbal tones instead of hops. Came off like a fruit gose."

"Tart, peach lemonade-y."

"The more you have the better it gets."

"What the holy fuck? No lacto, no Brett, no hops, sour goodness. I want it always . . ."

BLACK ADDER

At our brewery, Earth Eagle Brewings, we are tucked away in Northern New England, where the seasons are clearly defined—all eight of them. As the temperature drops and the leaves turn bright colors, we start thinking about, and eventually start brewing, darker beers. Before the reign of lagers and pilsners, dark beer was far more common, and among the first styles to become commercially produced and shipped.

Black Adder is a milk or cream stout, characterized by low gravity and the addition of lactose or milk sugar, a carbohydrate that beer yeast can't ferment. The lactose remains in the beer, adding body without making it super sweet. Milk stouts originated in the UK during the late 1800s, became the region's favorite stout by the early 1900s and reached their height of popularity after World War II, "touted as a healthy drink for lactating mothers and athletes in training," according to Mendel and Villa in the *Oxford Companion to Beer*. But as you might expect, we won't be making a traditional stout here, rather a stout/gruit hybrid. We'll use some hops at wort-in and flame-out, but they play more of a supportive role to the roasty malt flavors and two herbs: Labrador tea and star anise.

As previously mentioned, Labrador tea and wild rosemary often get confused. Labrador tea is a sub-species of wild rosemary. I have not detected a big difference in taste between them but Labrador tea is regarded as the less potent of the two. To further confuse things, an article in the *Journal of the Science of Food and Agriculture* reported that Labrador tea also refers to an actual tea comprised of *R. groenlandicum* and a few other closely related plants. "Labrador tea, called 'the grandmother of herbal teas,' has been drunk by Native Americans, Inuits and Canadian First Nations (Athabaskans, Cree) . . ."

In the 1600s, French-Canadian fur trappers, or the coureur des bois, mixed Labrador tea in with their supplies of black tea to make it last longer. "During the American War of Independence the leaves were much used instead of tea-leaves." M. Grieve goes on to say that placing the leaves in your clothes will keep away moths, and tossing some branches in your grains will keep out the mice. As with most of our herbal ingredients, Labrador tea is also toxic in large amounts. Dizziness, cramping and gnarly headaches are a clear sign you've overdone it—and that's just from too much strong tea. While we have had Labrador tea foraged for us before, we are several hours south of the boreal swamps and forests it grows in, so it's much easier to procure it from a few trusted Internet sources.

The grandmother of herbal teas: Labrador tea   *Star anise seed pods*

The fruit of *Illicium velum* tree, called star anise, provides an unusual and wondrous flavor that stimulates the appetite and digestion. The dried star-shaped pod and the seeds within them are what we're after, and unless you find yourself in Vietnam or China, you'll be foraging for this at your local health food store or on the Internet. Star anise possesses antibacterial and antifungal properties. It's also used to ease stomach pain and flatulence, and for respiratory issues like bronchitis and rheumatism. Because it is rich in shikimic acid, the vast majority of the star anise harvest is used in the production of the antiviral drugs like Tamiflu.

You'll be familiar with it if you enjoy Anisette, pastis or absinthe, as it is a key ingredient in all. Star anise is also one of the ingredients in garam masala and Chinese five-spice powder. The main flavor compound is anethole, which is also found in fennel, anise seed (a different plant) and most familiarly, licorice—the common default taste descriptor. Side-by-side, however, all these flavors are indeed different. Be sure to avoid Japanese star anise (*Illicium anisatum*), which is toxic in any amount.

BLACK ADDER

YIELD: 5 GALLONS (18.9 L), ALL-GRAIN

6 lb (2.72 kg) 2-row

5.5 lb (2.45 kg) Maris Otter

7 oz (198 g) chocolate malt

7 oz (198 g) special b

3.6 oz (102 g) flaked barley

3.6 oz (102 g) black patent malt

3.6 oz (102 g) c-60

3.6 oz (102 g) roasted barley

3.6 oz (102 g) wheat malt

Total Grain Bill: 14 lb (6.35 kg)

Mash Water: 4.22 gallons (16 L)

Sparge Water: 3.90 gallons (14.76 L)

Mash Temperature: 151°F (66°C)

Sparge Water Temperature: 168°F (76°C)

Boil Time: 1 hour

HERBS, ETC.*

1 oz (28 g) first wort East Kent Goldings hops

8 oz (227 g) milk sugar (lactose)

(or another low alpha acid hop)

1.5 oz (42.5 g) @ flame-out (f/o) Labrador tea, dried

0.2 oz (5.7 g) @ flame-out (f/o) star anise

½ oz (14 g) @ flame-out (f/o) Green Bullet hops

(or another high alpha hop)

YEAST

Wyeast West Yorkshire Ale #1469

Target OG: 1.067

Target FG: 1.016

ABV: 6.7%

Add the low alpha hops at first wort. At 30 minutes, draw off a quart or so of the wort into a small pot, slowly but thoroughly stir in the lactose so as not to oxygenate and then slowly pour the mix back into your wort. Lactose will not contribute positively to the beer if is clumped up and lying at the bottom of your kettle getting scorched.

Break up the Labrador tea leaves and bag. If you managed to find fresh leaves, cut them up with scissors, bag and then bruise by firmly rubbing and squeezing the bag. You'll want at least an additional half ounce than if dried. Star anise comes in powdered and whole forms, and as with coffee, grinding just before use seems to yield a greater amount of flavor than the pre-ground stuff. First, crush the pods and seeds between two cutting boards or carefully with a hammer ensuring that the pieces don't go flying around the room (see bash-box description in Chaga Groove, page 54). Put the pieces in a coffee grinder and process until they become a chunky powder. Add to the Labrador tea bag.

Note: Amounts are for dried herb. If fresh, double the amounts. Cut up the leaf and flowers, place in a muslin bag and bruise the herb by squeezing and rubbing the bag vigorously.

(continued)

Add the herbs at flame-out, along with a higher alpha hop such as Green Bullet. Keep immersed through ten-plus-minute whirlpool and ten-plus-minute settle for at least twenty minutes of total contact time.

While hot wort extracts some of the flavors/constituents, alcohol will extract others. You may want to "dry hop" with a portion of the Labrador tea. One of its more powerful constituents, ledum oil, is not soluble in water so a post-fermentation addition would make use of the alcohol present in the beer. If you decide to do this, put a sterilized weight, like a tri-clamp, in the bag to ensure maximum contact with the wort. Don't forget to take it out when you toss the bag!

After you have brewed this and feel like you have a sense of the basic beer, do tweak it. Consider switching out the star anise for fennel, anise seed, licorice root or maybe something completely different. As you'll see in the tasting notes, this group of flavors is pretty divisive. Wild rosemary is, of course, a great substitute for Labrador tea, but any number of medium-strength herbs such as spikenard or sweet fern would be an interesting variation.

Like most darker beers, Black Adder ages quite well in oak barrels, and we've also had good results with bourbon. Let it ride for between one and four months—well worth the wait!

TASTING NOTES

Brewer's Note: *Thin beige head on dark black liquid. Nose is chocolate, roast and mild lactose. Flavor has chocolate in front, light coffee licorice and lactose sweetness on the back. Balanced herbal bitterness, smooth silky mouthfeel.*

ONLINE BEER REVIEWS

Untappd.com Members

"This is real nice. Smooth stout with anise."

"Gruit stout with licorice . . . great combo."

"Great flavors. Really tasted the anise seed."

"Not a sweet stout. Anise plays nicely in this beer and gives it a certain bite."

"Labrador tea is very prominent."

"Great licorice nose, and you get the same in the taste. Could use a little more sweet or substance after the anise. But interesting."

"Not sure who gave this less than 4 stars . . . This is the first brew I've tried with anise. Good stuff."

POP! IPA

IPAs are arguably the antithesis of gruit beer—an expression of just one plant, modern brewing's default bittering/flavoring agent and its plethora of variations. Use of hops eventually brought the demise of gruit beer, but it wasn't because hops were "better" in beer than other plants. The shift was more about the quest for wealth and power amidst changing religious and economic trends in fourteenth and fifteenth centuries in Europe. Certainly folks continued to brew with other herbs in more isolated rural areas, but by and large brewing with anything other than hops became illegal in many countries. Great—more rules to break!

Almost every brewery in the United States has at least one IPA, and most have several versions. They continue to be the most sought-after style and show no sign of relenting, despite the IPA fatigue of many beer enthusiasts. And let's not forget: When properly brewed, they taste really good. We know this first-hand at Earth Eagle; our IPAs out-sell everything else we brew. So I couldn't help myself—the bull's-eye was right there. There had to be some way to take the new king of beers and "put the gruit to it." I suspected there were lots of herbs that could handle their own with a big hop charge—and I was right. It was just about then, early spring three years ago, that our intrepid forager Jenna asked if I'd be interested in brewing with poplar buds. One wonderful whiff and I knew I wanted to put them up against the pernicious weed.

Recently, Alex, my business partner and the architect of our hopped brews, said, yet again, "You know, hops are an herb too." Okay, I knew that, but it dawned on me that my occasional hop-forward brews could be more than subversive takes on the hallowed style—they could be yet another direction in brewing. Around then I came across ads for, and then drank, some amazing dry-hopped sours from other breweries and it was clear this was becoming a "thing"—hops were going where they had not been before.

POP! IPA features the delightfully aromatic, resinous, sticky buds of the poplar tree, also referred to as cottonwood. The primary North American tree is *Populus candicans*, but there are other useful varieties including *Populus nigra*, *P. canadensis* and *P. tacamahaca*. "Given the liberal sexual behavior of Cottonwoods, which freely interbreed with members of related species, it is sometimes very difficult to determine exactly which type of Poplar a given bud is derived from," according to Crystal Aneira of herbalriot.com. The Old World term "Balm of Gilead" is another name for poplar buds, but also refers to buds from other related and unrelated trees. Biblical references are most likely *Commiphora gileadensis*, an evergreen found in Africa and Asia. This term is also used for a prized balm used both medicinally and as a perfume, one of the gifts the Queen of Sheba gave to King Solomon.

"Balsam poplar or cottonwood is one of the most sacred trees in Native American plant lore. Many tribes regard them as a kind of spirit conductor, which conveys messages of the spirit world through their rustling leaves. Sacred objects, like the Hopi Kachinas, were fashioned from cottonwood. Cottonwoods were associated with fertility. In European plant lore, poplars are considered protective, especially against lightning and against snakes," states Aneira.

Typically the buds, or more specifically the pungent oil they contain, are used topically for skin care and muscle aches as well as internally in cough remedies. It contains salicin, which is converted into salicylic acid (essentially aspirin) by our liver and has many helpful properties including pain and inflammation relief. Bees collect it to produce propolis, and the Anishinabe Ojibwe Indians use it to enhance dreaming, among other applications, reported Matthew Wood. Consuming products with poplar bud should be avoided while pregnant.

The harvesting of these buds in late winter/early spring kicks off our foraging season. They are cone-shaped and pointed, about 2 centimeters long and 2 to 5 millimeters wide. Close up, you'll see glossy-brown scales that become sticky with resin as they warm up. For that reason, it is best to harvest them while it's still below freezing. They are at their most potent during this time and begin to decline as temperatures rise. Keep them frozen until your brew day. If you are out foraging, ideally you'll come across some winter casualties in a poplar grove, some downed branches or even trees. Rather than picking buds off standing trees, which will decrease the amount of leaves it can grow, look over what has fallen first. Along with some bitterness, this addition is going to add some forest for a bottom note, balsamic middle notes particularly in the smell, and a wee bit of vanilla and honey on top.

The point here is to introduce/strengthen the legitimacy of this hybridized beer, combining a strong addition of hops with other, equally potent herbs. It's a bit of a conundrum at our bar where typically half of the beers pouring are hopped and the other are typically not at all. We've called these beers "hopped gruits," but maybe there's another term out there that would do this more justice.

POP! IPA

YIELD: 5 GALLONS (18.9 L), ALL-GRAIN

5 lb (2.27 kg) maris otter

4.13 lb (1.87 kg) domestic 2-row

2.25 lb (1.02 kg) munich malt

6.6 oz (187 g) wheat malt

4 oz (113 g) special b

4 oz (113 g) aromatic

2.6 oz (74 g) c-60

2.6 oz (74 g) c-40

Total Grain Bill: 12.5 lb (5.7 kg)

Mash Water: 4.3 gallons (16.28 L)

Sparge Water: 3.7 gallons (14.01 L)

Mash Temperature: 151°F (66°C)

Mash Time: 75 minutes

Sparge Water Temperature: 168°F (76°C)

Boil Time: 1 hour

HERBS, ETC.*

1.5 oz (42.5 g) @ 60 minutes high alpha (such as Summit)

2 oz (57 g) ½ @ 30 minutes, ½ @ 10 minutes middle alpha (such as Zythos)

1.1 oz (31 g) 0.3 oz (9 g) @ 10 minutes, 0.8 oz (23 g) post-fermentation poplar buds

3.4 oz (96 g) post-fermentation middle alpha (such as Falconer's Flight)

YEAST

Wyeast American Ale #1056

Target OG: 1.061

Target FG: 1.010

ABV: 6.7%

While all of the recipes in this book are offered as springboards rather than dogmatic follow-this-recipe-or-else prescriptions, this one is really loose. You probably already have a fave IPA recipe, so feel free to ditch this one and use it. That being said, add your high alphas at 60 minutes and 1 ounce (28 g) of the mediums at 30 minutes. Add 0.3 ounces (8.5 g) of your poplar buds and the rest of your medium hops at 10 minutes. Store the remaining buds in a freezer. Four to five days before you cold-crash your fermenter, add the rest of your hops along with the rest of the buds. Nelson Sauvin or Sorachi Ace hops also make great finishing hops here.

Another variable to exploit when bending IPAs is yeast. You are probably in the habit of using a neutral yeast so as not to compete with and really showcase hop flavors, but let's not leave it at that. Experiment, play and dare to fool around with the tried and true. You might not wind up with something that you can even call an IPA, but you most likely will have a very interesting and enjoyable quaff.

After successfully using poplar buds, I've done variations with sweet gale, kava kava and sweet fern. Each one melded well with hops to yield a new and delicious hybrid. I suspect we're just on the tip of this humulus-bending iceberg.

Note: Amounts are for dried herb. If fresh, double the amounts. Cut up the leaf and flowers, place in a muslin bag and bruise the herb by squeezing and rubbing the bag vigorously.

(continued)

TASTING NOTES

Brewer's Note: *Honey gold, frothy head. Nose is fragrant—pine, minty herbal and a touch of citrus hops. Mouthfeel is light-medium in body. Notes of grapefruit, flowers, caramel with bitter citrus rind, hay funk, grape lollipop. Bitter sassafras on the finish, hint of bark flavor without hurting the hops. Light herbal lingering bitterness. Smooth.*

ONLINE BEER REVIEWS

BeerAdvocate.com Members

"Nose is extremely fragrant—medicinal, herbal and minty. Taste is all perfume and there's some bubblegum notes. Mouthfeel is light-medium in body with an even carbonation."

Untappd.com Members

"Light on pine . . . not on flavor."

"Amazing!"

"Surprisingly good."

"Must be the start of spring if this is on the menu."

"Hay funk grape lollipop, bitter citrus rind, dank with a tiny hint of sour. So fucking weird."

"Not very hoppy, but it is very good."

"Very unique."

"A nicely bitter brew."

"Poplar, dandelion, spruce, burdock, yep :-). Odd aroma but tastes really good; lingering bitter finish."

"Cool hoppy gruit. Unlike anything I have had—good stuff."

"Malty IPA . . . Dale's Pale Ale with a journey to find it."

"Pretty good IPA that gives a little tickle on the tongue like Pop Rocks."

"One of my favorite all time IPAs. Grapefruit floral up front, bitter sassafras on the finish. Hint of bark flavor without hurting the hop array."

"Mosiac, light herbal lingering bitterness."

"Great IPA—not as much citrus hoppy that I usually like . . . But it's a solid IPA."

"Unfiltered foamy copper. Good floral and earth hop notes. Smooth."

"Pretty solid fruity-hop forward IPA."

CHINESE ROCK

Alex and I have always had an affinity for Dogfish Head Brewery's constant experimentation and innovation with their beers. Their World Wide Stout was a catalyst for this beer—a high-gravity ale thanks to a big sugar bump. Using sugar was also compelling because of its use in Colonial-era beer; most were made without any grain whatsoever.

I was marveling at the different types of sugar in our local Asian market one day and came across something called Chinese rock sugar. It was literally beer-colored rocks of sugar poking holes through the plastic bag. I'm a big Ramones fan, so you might know where this is going. How could we not brew a beer called Chinese Rock? And while we're at it, why not brew a gruit version of it for our first home brew? So we skipped the hops and subbed in other herbs, and as mentioned earlier, it was magnificent out of the carboy. I got this weird chill down my spine when we realized it actually tasted very good, a premonition of sorts. We were off to the races!

We've covered all the relevant herbs here in previous recipes except for juniper (*Juniperus communis*), one of the preeminent and timeless gruit ingredients. Juniper grows in more places around the world than any other conifer. In most places, it grows as a small tree; however, in New England it's a small ground-hugging shrub. (If you come across a juniper shrub in Europe, however, avoid it as it's most likely the poisonous *Juniperus sabina*.) It sports short, rugged needles that can pierce the skin if handled roughly. What are popularly referred to as juniper berries are actually cones, as in spruce or pinecones. These juniper cones happen to have merged and quite fleshy scales, rather than the woody, clearly defined scales of other evergreens. Another brew-friendly version is the Eastern red cedar (*Juniperus virginiana*). These grow as small trees and in addition to needle foliage, mature branches also have overlapping scale-like leaves.

Juniper is held in high esteem by many cultures for its spiritual qualities, specifically as a protector from bad people, energies and occurrences such as accidents, theft and wild animal attacks. Needled branches are often burned ceremonially, which unleashes their antibiotic powers on any unsavory bacteria that might be in the air. Buhner wrote:

Juniper, tree of youthfulness, ever green   *Chocolate malt—no chocolate added*

A favorite food of many game birds as well as the primary constituent of gin, juniper berries produce a bitter somewhat piney flavor combined with a bit of fruitiness and pepperiness. They're used medicinally by herbalists to address a dizzying array of complaints, from water retention and flatulence to poor circulation and respiratory congestion. While it is said to increase male potency, it should not be used by those with kidney disease or during pregnancy!

A few years after our initial brew, I was cogitating on this recipe. It was just after Christmas, and we had some interesting food hanging around . . . namely a few loaves of raisin hobo bread and a jar of pickled pumpkin strips. BOOM! People brewed beer with bread thousands of years ago—some still do—so why not? The pickled pumpkin? Well, it did taste oddly good. We chopped it up, broke up the loaves of dark fruitcake and tossed it into the boil kettle, at about 30 minutes. That version was a stunner, and a big deal at the Portsmouth Beer Week Fest that year.

Finally, this beer has occasionally gone sour on us. Our house bugs, most likely invited by a stressed yeast pitch, delivered a version that was really unusual, essentially a sour stout. I must say, I'm not a big sour stout fan but this was *très* drinkable!

CHINESE ROCK

YIELD: 5 GALLONS (18.9 L), ALL-GRAIN

10.3 lb (4.67 kg) 2-row

1.43 lb (650 g) munich

15.2 oz (431 g) chocolate

6.3 oz (179 g) carafa III

2.5 oz (71 g) black patent

2.5 oz (71 g) C-120

2.5 oz (71 g) roasted barley

Total Grain Bill: 13.54 lb (6.14 kg)

Mash Water: 4.23 gallons (16 L)

Sparge Water: 3.89 gallons (14.7 L)

Mash Temperature: 151°F (66°C)

Mash Time: 60 minutes

Sparge Water Temperature: 168°F (76°C)

Boil Time: 75 minutes

HERBS, ETC.*

1.5 lb (680 g) 30 minutes lump rock candy or sugar

1 oz (28 g) @ ½ 30 minutes, ½ flame-out (f/o) juniper berries (ground), divided

0.4 oz (11 g) @ ½ 15 minutes, ½ flame-out (f/o) sweet gale

0.4 oz (11 g) @ ½ 15 minutes, ½ flame-out (f/o) wild rosemary

8 oz (227 g) post-fermentation sugar (rock, coconut, palm, brown, Belgian, etc.)

YEASTS

Belgian Ale (Wyeast #1214) in primary

Champagne (Lalvin Champagne EC-1118 packet) in secondary

Target OG: 1.067

Target FG: 1.010

ABV: 7.5+%

Around 30 minutes into the boil, if you're using lump or rock sugar, break it up into small, pea-sized pieces so you do not find undiluted sugar in your trub. Also take half of your juniper berries and process them in a coffee grinder until they are coarsely powdered. Add sugar and berry powder to a metal cooking pot and draw off enough hot wort to cover the mix. Slowly stir until the ingredients are fully diluted. Be careful not stir or whisk too fast, as adding oxygen into your wort will degrade flavors. Slowly pour the mix back into your kettle. This is a good time to add any bread, fruitcake or pickled or dried fruit if you're going deep. Break up a half a loaf into thumb-sized pieces, chop up a heaping handful of pickled pumpkin-or-whatever, bag it and toss into the boil.

Note: Amounts are for dried herb. If fresh, double the amounts. Cut up the leaf and flowers, place in a muslin bag and bruise the herb by squeezing and rubbing the bag vigorously.

(continued)

Bag half of your sweet gale and wild rosemary, bruise the contents a bit, and then add the bag at fifteen minutes. Wild rosemary can be substituted with Labrador tea. Take some time to make sure the contents are fully saturated either by repeatedly dipping it or holding it beneath the surface with a clean spoon or other utensil. Occasionally pull the bag out, let most of the liquid drain back into the kettle and then put the bag back. This helps to draw out more of the flavor into your wort, just like you'd do with a tea bag.

Combine the rest of your herbs in another bag, bruise and then add the remaining juniper berry powder to it. Add to the kettle at flame-out, again making sure the contents are fully saturated. Keep immersed through ten-plus-minute whirlpool and ten-plus-minute settle for at least twenty minutes of total contact time. This second bag can then be added into the fermenter to further enhance flavor. Discard the first bag. If you decide to do this, make sure all areas of the herb bags have been sterilized by contact with hot wort. Put a sterilized weight, like a tri-clamp, in the bag to ensure maximum contact with the wort. Don't forget to take it out when you toss the bag!

TASTING NOTES

Brewer's Note: *Deep dark brown, nearly opaque, thin head dissipates quickly. Spicy in the nose, ginger, nutmeg, licorice, sarsaparilla. Taste nutmeg, anise, allspice, cola, tea leaves, juniper berry and Christmas spice with dark malty chewiness. Body medium, carbonation was medium to low, alcohol well-hidden. Light sweetness in the finish with some mellow chocolate.*

ONLINE BEER REVIEWS

BeerAdvocate.com Member
"Lots of spice in the nose; maybe ginger, nutmeg, licorice and sarsaparilla, to name a few. Taste was rich and quite unique, even compared to other gruits I've had. Body was about medium, and quite appropriately so, carbonation was medium to low, the higher alcohol was quite well-hidden. A very interesting brew overall, and one of the best I've had from the state of New Hampshire."

Untappd.com Members

"SO hard to describe. Sour? Dry? Tea-ish? Try for something different."

"Very complex . . . phenomenal!"

"So good. Sweet flavor hidden in there that I can't place."

"Interesting . . . would pair well with spicy Asian food."

"Lindsey hated this beer. I fucking loved it. Nice sour stout. Lots of flavors going on. Too drunk to explain it. Just drink this beer."

GALLOWS HARVEST

We've delighted in re-creating several historic recipes, often from arcane journals and other publications unearthed by our collaborator, Emerson "Tad" Baker, professor of history at Salem State University. Sometimes we attempt to follow these recipes to the letter and other times we have taken some liberties. Either way the resulting beers are all liquid time machines of varying degrees, a real thrill providing you get something drinkable. Gallows Harvest debuted a few years ago at Cambridge Brewing Company's wonderful Great Pumpkin Festival to commemorate Professor Baker's book *A Storm of Witchcraft*. A key inspiration for the recipe was an early New England ballad titled Forefather's Song, which is thought to be from the early 1630s—around the time New England began to be settled. Part of the next to the last stanza goes as follows:

OUR PUMPKINS AND PARSNIPS ARE COMMON SUPPLIES;

WE HAVE PUMPKINS AT MORNING AND PUMPKINS AT NOON,

IF IT WAS NOT FOR PUMPKINS WE SHOULD BE UNDONE!

IF BARLEY BE WANTING TO MAKE INTO MALT,

WE MUST BE CONTENTED, AND THINK NO FAULT;

FOR WE CAN MAKE LIQUOR TO SWEETEN OUR LIPS,

OF PUMPKINS AND PARSNIPS AND WALNUT-TREE CHIPS . . .

One of the fun and inspiring things about this time is that brewers used anything and everything they could find to make beer, as the excerpt attests. Shipments of beer and brewing supplies from England were inconsistent at best so these folks became quite inventive. Another factor was that people from European cities were accustomed to drinking beer, not water, because the water where they came from was often undrinkable. As a result, many of these settlers were suspicious of the pristine New World waters; they wanted their beer! Historian Greg Smith, in his book *Beer in America*, wrote:

> More than a mere cultural habit, beer drinking evolved into a healthful practice. Brewers boiled water to make beer, thus killing the microbes that imperil health. In Europe, fouled drinking water placed city dwellers in peril; those who used the fetid supply regularly developed serious health problems. . . . There, rivers and streams were becoming the equivalents of flowing dumps.

Gallows is a mishmash of old recipes, many of which include sage, and many other old world cure-alls like blessed thistle, spikenard, wood betony and gentian root. Since our local farmers' markets are stuffed with squash of all kinds in the fall (and since we already had a very popular pumpkin beer, Puca), we brewed with other squash instead.

The very bitter gentian root (*Gentiana lutea*), also known as yellow gentian, grows in alpine and sub-alpine areas of Europe and enjoys a long history in various beverages. Although it provides many benefits, it's best known for its ability to stimulate the appetite and digestive juices. Perhaps its most famous use in these parts is the peculiar soft-drink called Moxie. It also figures prominently in Aperol, an Italian liqueur as well as Angostura bitters, to name just a few. *G. puberula*, *G. saponaria* and *G. andrewsii* are cited as American substitutes by M. Grieve, and Buhner mentions *Swertia radiata* as well. Roots are harvested in the fall and slowly dried.

Wood betony (*Stachys Betonica*) is found in Europe, western Asia and northern Africa. Some sources site a North American analog called lousewort (*Pedicularis canadensis*), however this does not seem to enjoy the vast applications of its European cousin. Wood betony was seen as a panacea by many ancient cultures in both the physical as well as the spiritual world according to M. Grieve. She quotes Apuleius, who in Roman times wrote, "It is good whether for the man's soul or for his body; it shields him against visions and dreams, and the wort is very wholesome." Betony has "a strong influence on the stomach . . . and on the brain, head and nervous system generally, improving gut-level instincts, thinking and groundedness," reported Matthew Wood. It's a muscle relaxant which, when added to a beer, "enhances the relaxant properties of alcohol, producing a highly effective ale for nervous stress," according to Buhner.

Described as a "plant of great virtue," blessed thistle (*Cnicus benedictus*) is a transplant to North America from Europe. Legend has it that while at war in the 1200s, the Scots were alerted to a Danish raid when one of the Danes, bare-footed to avoid detection, stepped on the spikey-leaved plant and cried out in pain. From dizziness to joint pain, digestive issues to menstrual pain, even deafness and depression, blessed thistle has got you covered. However, despite these truly impressive healing powers, it is often regarded as a mere invasive weed. Its pungent bitter flavor is a main constituent in Benedictine, a fascinating liqueur first produced by the

Squash in the mash tun

Gentian root

Benedictine monks in 1510, and contains a proprietary mix of 27 herbs. Ironically, it's very good for the liver as well. Prime harvesting time is in July, just as the plant starts to flower. As with any herb, it should be cut only after the morning dew has evaporated. The stalk, leaves and flowers are all usable.

While we previously mentioned sage flowers in the Bloomers chapter (page 44), this mighty herb merits a bit more attention. The Salvias, commonly known as sage, grow all over the world in hundreds of different varieties, with more than 500 in the Americas alone. *Salvia officinalis* is perhaps the most familiar for its culinary use with meat. *Salvia divinorum* may be the most notorious because of its psychoactive effects. Fortunately, most sage varieties are interchangeable in their effects and brew-ability, but do your homework. I recommend considering locally found varieties first, and it's the leaves we're after here. Sage is yet another powerful herb that has had a long relationship with humankind. "It [sage] possesses virtues almost too numerous to comprehend under a single heading," reported Wood. M. Grieve cited an old French saying: "Sage helps the nerves and by its powerful might, Palsy is cured and fever put to flight." During the Middle Ages, sage ale was popular and considered highly medicinal and wholesome according to Buhner. Art in the Age, an American distillery with an eye toward the past, makes a blithe 80 proof spirit simply called Sage.

GALLOWS HARVEST

YIELD: 5 GALLONS (18.9L), ALL-GRAIN

0.4 lb (181 g) parsnips, shredded

2.5 lb (1.13 kg) squash, shredded

2.5 oz (71 g) rice hulls

8.5 lb (3.86 kg) 2-row

1.5 lb (680 g) munich

1.5 lb (680 g) rye malt

1.4 lb (680 g) wheat malt

12 oz (340 g) flaked rice

2.5 oz (71 g) midnight wheat

2.5 oz (71 g) peat, smoked

Total Grain Bill: 17.6 lb (7.98 kg)

Mash Water: 4.2 gallons (15.9 L)

Sparge Water: 3.8 gallons (14.4 L)

Mash Temperature: 151°F (66°C)

Mash Time: 60 minutes

Sparge Water Temperature: 168°F (76°C)

Boil Time: 75 minutes

HERBS, ETC.*

9 oz (255 g) molasses

0.26 oz (7.4 g) @ 15 minute sage

0.2 oz (5.7 g) @ first wort low alpha hop (Vanguard)

0.36 oz (10.2 g) @ flame-out (f/o) blessed thistle

0.29 oz (8.2 g) @ flame-out (f/o) spikenard

0.29 oz (8.2 g) @ flame-out (f/o) wood betony

0.21 oz (6 g) @ flame-out (f/o) gentian

YEAST

West Yorkshire (Wyeast #1469)

Target OG: 1.069

Target FG: 1.016

ABV: 7%

The first thing is to wash and then process the squash and parsnips—and there are options. Over the years we have used ambercup, red kuri, blue hubbard and Hidatsa, but any squash with a pronounced taste is fair game. Remove any stems, cut the squash in half and then scrape out the guts and seeds. If you really want to get into this, you can separate the seeds, toast them and then grind them up for use in the mash or boil.

Leaving the skin on, cut the squash meat and parsnips into 1-inch (2.5-cm) cubes and decide whether you want to roast them in your oven with some maple syrup, purée, bag and add them to the boil or just shred them raw in a food processor and toss them loose into your mash. We do the latter.

Bag and break up the sage leaf for a fifteen-minute addition.

Note: Amounts are for dried herb. If fresh, double the amounts. Cut up the leaf and flowers, place in a muslin bag and bruise the herb by squeezing and rubbing the bag vigorously.

(continued)

Do the same with the other herbs for an addition at flame-out. They can all be added to the same bag provided there is enough room left over for the herbs to expand into. If not, use more bags. As usual, take some time to make sure the herb bags are fully saturated either by repeatedly dipping them or holding it beneath the surface with a clean spoon or other utensil. Occasionally pull the bag out, let most of the liquid drain back into the kettle and then put the bag back. This helps to draw out more of the flavor into your wort, just like you'd do with a tea bag. Keep immersed through ten-plus-minute whirlpool and ten-plus-minute settle for at least twenty minutes of total contact time.

TASTING NOTES

Brewer's Note: *Muddy chocolate soda, off-white head. Aroma is light toast, tart fruit, ginger, sage, squash, red berries, floral notes, sweetbread and toffee malt. Flavor is bready, more toffee malt with light spice, squash and tart fruit. The easygoing spiciness balances the lightly sweet malts. Dry finish with apple-like esters, white pepper, vanilla. Light body, low carbonation, a tad tart.*

ONLINE BEER REVIEWS

Untappd.com Members

"You can really taste the sage."

"Different, but not in a bad way."

"Whoa spice."

"It's different, the flavors are super interesting. Our first gruit!"

"Sweet yams and a spicy sage taste. A little sour to boot."

"Purrfect fall spice gruit."

"Enjoyably complex squash fruit."

"Like beer and Kombucha had a baby!"

"Great change of pace beverage."

"Strange. But good."

"A cornucopic blending of squash sour and herbs."

DRAKONIA

There is a familiar comfort in the cartoon version of Halloween: warted hags, dancing skeletons and grinning jack-o-lanterns. Perhaps you imagined this imagery when I mentioned the original home brewers in the beginning of this book? Well, the trick-or-treaters have all scurried home because this is where we get heavy. Drakonia is a nod to the times long before beer wound up on a corporate throne in the fluorescent-lit halls of modernity. In the shadows of the backwoods, times when science was joined with spirit and knowledge with direct experience, Druid and witch, shaman and alchemist brewed with powerful and teaching plants. Their intentions were not to provide people with a brief fizzy escape from the real world. Rather, their charge was to bring folks deeper into the real world, whether to address a physical illness, some mental issue or a spiritual malaise—all with the help and guidance of plants.

Although practically all the herbs presented in this book are dangerous in large amounts (not to mention alcohol!) the ones explored here are in their own class; they warrant extra care and respect. Once again I'll return to my safety mantra: We are after flavors, not psychedelic experiences. That said, there is a subtle realm of experience that merits mention. "To the attentive mind, all plants are psychotropic; they all change consciousness, awareness, understanding and sense of self," proclaimed Buhner.

Scotch heather or ling (*Calluna vulgaris* formerly *Erica vulgaris*) dominates the moors of the British Isles and Europe, and is a plant praised for its beauty as much as its use in beer. While it's native to those areas, it has been introduced to many others including North America. Heather was "despised until the 19th century for its associations with the most rugged rural poverty," according to the World Heritage Encyclopedia. The Scots didn't seem to feel this way, as they used the roots for knife handles, wore the plant's likeness as an emblem, and used the flowers and leaves in an intoxicating brew. According to the British conservation organization Trees For Life:

"But even before the Scots applied heather's many uses to various walks of life, the Picts were renowned for their heather ale. This drink has been made for many centuries in Scotland, and archaeologists have found traces of a fermented drink made of heather flowers on a 3,000 year old Neolithic shard of pottery on the Isle of Rum."

If you're not up on your Scottish history, the Picts inhabited Scotland before the invading Scots finally decimated them in 848 AD. They were a fierce people, small in stature, who got their name from the tattoos and body paints they reputedly adorned their bodies with. Their heather brew was renowned and also a closely guarded secret as illustrated in the poem "Heather Ale: A Galloway Legend" by Robert Louis Stevenson, wherein the last Pictish king finds death preferable over divulging the recipe to the Scottish invaders. Ironically, heather was thought to bring good fortune and protection. Some believe that the original heather ale was not an ale at all but rather a mead, a honey-based drink rather than barley-based, suggests Buhner. Others think it was made of heather alone and that the fermentables were provided by nectar from heather flowers. Oh, and it wasn't just the Picts and Scots who used it; early peoples throughout the north of Europe and Scandinavia included it in their brews.

Mandrake (*Atropa mandragora* formerly *Mandragora officinalis*) is certainly one of the most sacred of herbs, used for centuries in various cultures for medicine as well as in rituals and ceremonies. It's a member of the Solanaceae order, which includes everyday plants like potato and tomato, along with the mysterious Belladonna, Henbane and the Daturas. This long-living perennial, which originated in Mediterranean countries, grows thick sturdy roots that often resemble a human body. The Egyptians called it the phallus of the field, a nod to its aphrodisiac and fertility-aiding qualities. Somewhat controversial is the idea that Egyptians used mandrake in fermented beverages. A key supporting document was found to have a major translation error where the word for a certain mineral was mistaken for mandrake, reported The Poison Garden. There do, however, appear to be images of mandrake plants on various Egyptian objects from that time.

Buhner reported that the Latin meaning of *Atropa mandragora* is, "the dragon-mind that holds the shears that cut the thread of life," referring to its effects on consciousness in high concentrations. "Ancient Germanic peoples also made use of the plant, especially their seeresses, who were known for their clairvoyant abilities far outside of Europe. . . . The demonization of mandrake begun once Germany became dominated by Christianity," according to Entheology.com.

It was used by the ancient Greeks to knock people out before surgery and eaten by Rachel (of Biblical fame) so that she could conceive and give birth to Joseph. In Medieval times, folks would carry the root, called a manniken, for good luck in love, business and gambling, and as protector against evil spirits, spells or weapons. All of these attributes combined to make mandrake a very sought-after plant and, consequently, a very rare and often faked commodity. One of the charges against Joan of Arc was that she wore a manniken, according to Dale Pendell.

Heather   *Mandrake*

Important to note that so-called American mandrake (*Podophyllum peltatum*), also known as mayapple, is not what we're after. We did make a brown ale with mayapple root, by mistake, because we weren't paying attention to the Latin name. While the resulting ale was delicious, it had a rather pronounced laxative effect on some people—not recommended.

Although I have yet to brew with it because it is so difficult to source, henbane (*Hyoscyamus niger*) is another herbal heavyweight deserving of mention—and extreme caution. The priestesses of the Oracle of Delphi are rumored to have inhaled henbane smoke. According to anthropologist Christian Rätsch, Pilsenkraut was the name of a German beer in which henbane was used instead of hops. This changed in the nineteenth century when "the Czechs invented new brewing technique . . . using a special yeast and lots of hops producing beer with yellow color and bitter taste," that very beer style we are so saturated with today. "Rätsch warns not to have any more of the brew on hand than can be safely drunk without overdosing on the henbane, because henbane beer creates its own thirst and once you start, anything around will be drunk," reported Pendell.

DRAKONIA

YIELD: 5 GALLONS (18.9 L), ALL-GRAIN

9.07 lb (4.1 kg) 2-row
1.65 lb (758 g) Vienna
15.2 oz (430 g) flaked corn
11.2 oz (318 g) flaked rice
6.6 oz (187 g) crystal 120
6.6 oz (187 g) midnight wheat
Total Grain Bill: 13.2 lb (5.98 kg)

Mash Water: 4.53 gallons (17.15 L)
Sparge Water: 3.55 gallons (13.44 L)

Mash Temperature: 151°F (66°C)
Mash Time: 75 minutes
Sparge Water Temperature: 168°F (76°C)
Boil Time: 60 minutes

HERBS, ETC.*

0.6 oz (17 g) @ ½ 30 minutes, ½ 15 minutes
mandrake root
0.8 oz (23 g) @ 10 minutes heather flowers
0.8 oz (23 g) @ 10 minutes elder flowers

YEAST

London III (Wyeast #1318)

Target OG: 1.061
Target FG: 1.012
ABV: 6.4%

You'll want to break up the mandrake root as much as possible from its usual chunks of wood down to about malt grain-sized pieces. Be sure you have the right stuff too—double check the Latin name! Refer to the process and bash-box in the Chaga Groove chapter (page 54). Slowly mix the processed root with some hot wort in a metal pan and add back at the prescribed times. Definitely cover your nose and mouth as a lot of mandrake dust is produced, and huffing it is most likely a bad idea.

I have read that dried henbane leaf and/or crushed seeds can be substituted for the mandrake but again, I have not brewed with it yet and cannot personally vouch for the results. Too much of this stuff can actually be deadly, so unless you've done your homework—don't bother. I have, however, subbed out the heather and elder with motherwort, brahmi and sweet fern in similar amounts, resulting in a somewhat sweeter, fruitier tasting beer. Some of the comments below are from that batch.

Bag and bruise the other herbs per usual before adding, making sure each bag is thoroughly saturated.

Note: Amounts are for dried herb. If fresh, double the amounts. Cut up the leaf and flowers, place in a muslin bag and bruise the herb by squeezing and rubbing the bag vigorously.

TASTING NOTES

Brewer's Note: *Amber color with a spicy/earthy nose. Somewhat sweet earthy flavors with fruit notes, interesting mid range flavors, mugwort, fennel. A tad tart, lightly carbonated. Complex flavor-wise but smooth drinking and unique.*

ONLINE BEER REVIEWS

Untappd.com Members

"Gruit beer. Very nice sweet flavor. Love it!"

"Amber gruit with mandrake. A little buttery. It reminds me a bit of a popcorn ball."

"Sweet taste and good fruit notes."

"Love the smell far more than the taste."

"High marks for its drinkability. Could use more character or intensity."

"Yum—very interesting mid range flavors. Maybe that happens with gruits when you remove hops?"

"Glorious infusion of herbal glory!"

"Amber gruit that I am really enjoying. Well-balanced."

"Whoa, this is good. An amber gruit with good flavor and body."

"Tart, lightly carbonated; got a lot going on flavor-wise but fairly smooth drinking."

"Great intro to gruits—so many unique, drinkable flavors not found elsewhere in the usual styles."

"The flavors struggle to work together. It tastes good, but it's a little confusing."

PORTER COCHON

In 2011, Michigan's Right Brain Brewery won a gold medal for Best Experimental Beer at the Great American Beer Festival. That beer, Mangalitsa Pig Porter, was brewed with Mangalitsa pig heads and bones—the thought of which just blew our minds. A few days after an excited discussion about this with my partner and some of our home brew buddies, I received a call. "Hey, Butch, this is Tony. I have a line on a pig head, when do you want it?" What?! I didn't remember saying anything about wanting to actually brew such a beer but, gulp, opportunity was a knockin'. We reluctantly took delivery of a 27-pound (12-kg) pig head from Canada. Jean Claude, the deceased suid, had reportedly enjoyed a very happy life with his sister Antoinette and seemed to have a smile on his face when he, or rather his head, arrived.

As it turns out, there are precedents for meat beer starting in seventeenth-century England with a winsome brew called Cock Ale. The first printed recipe for it appears to have been published by the Englishman Sir Kenelm Digby (1603–1665). A specially cooked and prepared rooster was put in a muslin bag and tossed into fermenting beer. In "The Young Gallants Tutor, Or, An Invitation to Mirth," a rather lusty song from the 1670s, an anonymous author celebrates several particular beverages: "With love and good liquor our hearts we do cheer, Canary and Claret, Cock Ale and March beer." Women bemoaned the "Decay of that true Old English Vigour" caused by the excess consumption of coffee. They lamented that English men had formerly been "the Ablest Performers in Christendome," but "our Gallants being every way so Frenchified . . . they are become meer Cock-sparrows," as written in The Women's Petition Against Coffee. The good ladies then suggest outlawing coffee and "returning to the good old strengthning Liquors of our Forefathers," which included, yes, Cock Ale, a "Lusty nappy Beer." Oh and yes, we brewed up a batch with a rooster and two hens at Earth Eagle and it was a fantastic beer!

Fast-forward to 1940s Britain and grab a pint of Mercer's Meat Stout, advertised with the mottos "Tastes good, does you good," and "When in doubt, take meat stout!" This rather unusual beer was one of the many foodstuffs created for invalids and "persons of weak digestion." By adding a meat extract to the beer, folks who had trouble physically eating meat got to drink it instead. Oyster stout is said to have originated around this time as well. Michael Jackson cited the now defunct Hammerton Brewery in London as having added "oyster concentrate" to a few batches of their oatmeal stout before it went bad—none of it ever made it to market.

Blood from smoking boar's heads *Arranging heads in the smoker*

Currently we are blessed with beers that have been brewed with bull testicles, whale meat, insects, coffee beans via elephant intestines and, of course, the ubiquitous bacon beers. At Earth Eagle, we've brewed with bear meat, beef bones, beef and pig offal, as well as boar and moose heads—all of which were eagerly consumed by our intrepid customers. I must acknowledge that there are scores of brewers, and drinkers too, who detest such beery abominations—and they certainly have a right to their opinions. However, from over here on the arty side of the spectrum, I say brew with whatever you want and if it tastes good, drink it.

Even though we aren't making dinner here, I always like to consider herbs you would cook the particular meat with. I'll also think about what grows in the habitat of said animal if it's wild. We've covered sage previously (page 44), so let's consider the popular Asian spice lemongrass (*Cymbopogon citratus*). Part of the grass family, lemongrass possesses a myriad of helpful qualities. It helps relieve pain of all sorts, helps ease depression and boosts self-esteem. It's antimicrobial, antibacterial and ironically, is a galactogogue: It increases the production and quality of milk for lactating mothers—and that's not nearly all. This India native boosts the strength of connective tissues and immune functions, according to Matthew Wood. Lemongrass is used for magical purposes in both Hoodoo and Mexican folk magic traditions, primarily as a cleansing agent for negative energies. It lends a very pleasant lemon flavor without the sourness of actual lemon.

Sweet gale and sweet fern twig smoke

Quite boaring!

We've used the flowers of culinary lavender (*Lavandula angustifolia* or *L. munstead*) in this recipe. The first recorded uses of lavender occur thousands of years ago in Egypt—as part of the mummification process. Fast-forward several centuries to the Great Plague of 1665. Lavender was used in four thieves vinegar, a preparation used by grave robbers to wash their hands and ward off infection, reported M. Grieve. A curious theme here, right?

On a brighter note, its scent has been shown to elevate moods and help to alleviate mild agitation and anxiety. There are many other varieties of this herb used in soaps, cosmetics and perfumes—not what we want. Even the right stuff in a beer is a bit daring as too much will leave your brew bitter and smelling like your grandma's bathroom. It is rumored that 10 percent of folks taste lavender as soapy and plain unsavory, as with cilantro. For that remaining 90 percent, using the right amount adds another dimension to this already wildly complex collection of scents and tastes. Specifically, lavender adds a subtly sweet floral flavor with citrus notes.

PORTER COCHON

YIELD: 5 GALLONS (18.9 L), ALL-GRAIN

8.25 lb (3.7 kg) 2-row

2 lb (907 g) munich

13.5 oz (383 g) amber

7 oz (198 g) flaked barley

7 oz (198 g) carafa 1

3 oz (85 g) chocolate malt

Total Grain Bill: 12.15 lb (5.5 kg)

Mash Water: 3.82 gallons (14.5 L)

Sparge Water: 4 gallons (15 L)

Mash Temperature: 151°F (66°C)

Mash Time: 60 minutes

Sparge Water Temperature: 168°F (76°C)

Boil Time: 90 minutes

HERBS, ETC.*

1 pig or boar head, skinned/smoked

0.4 oz (11 g) @ ½ 30 minutes, ½ 10 minutes +/-13% alpha hops

0.3 oz (8.5 g) @ ½ 30 minutes, ½ 10 minutes sage

0.3 oz (8.5 g) @ ½ 30 minutes, ½ 10 minutes lemongrass

0.1 oz (3 g) @ 10 minutes culinary lavender, optional

10 oz (283 g) @ 30 minutes Medjool dates, minced, optional

YEAST

Any American or British ale yeast

Target OG: 1.058

Target FG: 1.015

ABV: 5.6%

Meat beers are among the most arduous to brew—which is why we do them so infrequently. It's not a very pretty process either; if you have a weak stomach, you might skip this. The big thing to remember is that fat is a head-killer and will eventually turn rancid if not removed—more on that later. Porter Cochon starts a few days before the actual brew day. The steps for a 5-gallon (18.9-L) batch: thaw the head, skin it, smoke it, make a broth with it and then add half of that broth to your wort at flame-out. Assuming the head you are using is frozen, it will take at least 24 hours for it to thaw at room temperature. Then it's skinnin' time. Since the best meat on most mammals is from the head, the objective is to peel off the face without removing any meat. If you've never skinned anything before, get some help. It's not rocket science, but seeing it done once or twice helps a lot.

Note: Amounts are for dried herb. If fresh, double the amounts. Cut up the leaf and flowers, place in a muslin bag and bruise the herb by squeezing and rubbing the bag vigorously.

The next step is to smoke the skinned head in a conventional backyard smoker. We have used hickory and apple wood in the past but now use sweet gale and sweet fern stalks and twigs saved from previous brews, soaked in water. Plus or minus 2 hours of cool smoke at 150°F (66°C) or below does the trick. A fair amount of blood will drain during this process—if possible, collect it in a jar and refrigerate immediately. You'll want to add this later to your boil. Don't have a way to smoke? Mix up a good meat rub, heavy on the sugar, and apply it liberally. Then use a blow-torch to brown (caramelize) the head. Be careful not to burn it—or yourself. Gloves and safety glasses are a must.

Now is a good time to mention brains—you want the brains in your beer! This creamy and tasty substance should not be wasted and it will be, unless you take an extra few steps to liberate them. If you want to keep the skull looking good, drill several small holes in a circle on the back of it. Keeping it nose down, carefully knock out the disc of bone. Then, with a small whisk or even a chopstick, stir up the contents of the cavity into a liquid. Keep the skull in a nose-down position until use. If you'll be discarding the skull, just use a large drill bit and put a hole in the top of the skull, between the eyes a few inches away from the back of the skull. Be sure to stir 'em up after.

To make a broth, find a suitably sized pot and boil the head for 2 to 2½ hours in enough water to fully submerge it, nose up. Add a pint (473 ml) of honey or maple syrup or a half pint (237 ml) of each when the water comes to a boil to enhance the flavor. Then remove the head, strain out any meat and fat bits, and boil that broth some more until you have reduced it to plus or minus 1½ gallons (5.7 L). If you are picky about your brew numbers, be sure to adjust the brew day water volumes and gravity calculations to account for this liquid and sugar addition.

Next, let the broth cool and then put it in a freezer overnight. The next day you'll find a disc or at least some globules of hardened fat on top which you'll want to remove and discard (or save to cook with!). Be sure to get all the fat out before adding the broth to the wort at flame-out. If it's ice-cold when you add it, check the temp of your wort after the addition as you might not need to chill your wort further. Use half and freeze the rest for another batch, or soup stock. If you're a bit sensitive in the smell department, you will probably be overwhelmed by the smoke and meat vapors, enough to feel like this reduced broth will be too strong to add to your wort. Not so much. It's amazing how much stronger the malt flavors are by the time this beer makes it into a glass.

(continued)

If you will be scaling up the recipe, you may be able to skip the broth step. For a 2-barrel (65-gallon [246-L]) batch we use five heads, each in its own muslin bag. We tie off one end of a length of butcher's string to each bag and tie the other end to our kettle. Once the water hits 170°F (77°C), we lower the bags in and leave them suspended in the kettle for the entire boil, careful that none of them are touching the heating elements inside. We don't add any sugar here as the wort provides plenty. The potential challenge with this method, however, is fat removal. At the end of the boil it's all liquidized on top of the wort—a big oily slick of it. We simply stop the knock-out pump when it looks as though the wort is almost gone—right before that fat gets pumped into the fermenter. If you have a bottom port on your boil kettle, you can do the same. If not, you'll want to skim off the fat slick with a big shallow spoon before you knock out. Make sure you get it all.

And so comes the added bonus section of this recipe: face meat! Once your pig head cools, do take the time to pull/cut off as much of the meat as you can. Not sure you want to bother? Taste a piece—smoked meat cooked in that sweet wort—you know it's gonna be good! The cheeks and tongue are the best, just be sure to pull the outer skin off the tongue before eating. The rest of the meat can be ground up for use in sausage, head cheese or pâté. If you're not up to it, you probably know someone else who'd jump at the chance to use it. If you want to save the skull, you'll want to be extra thorough about the meat removal. There are plenty of resources on the Internet about next steps for getting a clean and stink-free skull that you can "employ decoratively" later on.

TASTING NOTES

Brewer's Note: *Smoky bacon jerky without being overpowering, dark malt tasty. Smooth on the tongue, clean finish, very approachable. Hints of salted, cured meats. Taste similar to the aroma, medium sweetness and dark roasted malts with slight coffee flavor. On the finish roasted coffee with light smoke. Medium bodied medium carbonation.*

ONLINE BEER REVIEWS

Untappd.com Members

"This deserves more stars. Smoky bacon jerky dark malt tasty. A carnivore's happy place."

"Solid smoked taste, very subtle. Smooth on the tongue, clean finish. Very approachable. Boar heads in beer? Doesn't even sound right. But despite that, it was a smoky beer that had a bacon aftertone. Great brew! Very unique."

"Great smoke flavor without being overpowering."

"Utterly bizarre, and that makes it wonderful. The best 'bacony' beer I've ever run across."

CONNIE FERALE

The use of evergreens in alcoholic drinks is probably as old as beer itself. Based on chemical analysis of pottery shards, McGovern posits that such drinks existed in the Neolithic Middle East—10,200 BC. He cites third-century Chinese poet Wang Ji, a member of the Seven Sages of the Bamboo Grove, who wrote of "a good drink made with pine needles and chrysanthemums." Scandinavian people have a long brewing history with juniper, although curiously many eschewed spruce and fir because they felt the resinous qualities too strong, according to Buhner. Indigenous Americans used spruce for coughs, colds and flu. Some made a spruce tea during the winter months to fight scurvy, a condition caused by a lack of vitamin C, which spruce tips happen to contain. This knowledge was picked up by colonists and sailors alike who began to brew beer with spruce to ward off scurvy.

Twigs and needles were also used in Colonial American beer when imported hops were scarce, as they imparted somewhat similar flavors as well as similar preservative qualities. Martyn Cornell wrote of a beer made from fermented spruce sap in 1664 London. He also cited a London newspaper ad printed a century later that seems to indicate that spruce beer was imported to Britain, offering "American spruce beer in the highest perfection."

While you can toss evergreen branches in a brew any time of year, the ideal time to brew this beer, or at least to forage these ingredients, is spring. Harvest spruce tips when they first start to come out of their brown papery casings at the end of each branch. The term "tip" is a bit misleading; bud is a bit more accurate. They are bright green, much brighter than the tree, and are at their most potent yielding citrus and slightly resinous notes. Using older growth will result in an additional bitterness and tanic notes. Budding pine tips are called pine candles because of their candle shape and the way they point upright toward the sky. They lend a slightly different version of resin and citrus.

Pine candles just starting to form

Fir, balsam and hemlock trees are also fair game, and each has its own slight taste variation. Moonlight Brewery in Santa Rosa, California, uses redwood tips in a sumptuous seasonal brew called Working for Tips. Several other breweries do spruce beers, but none of them are gruits as far as we know. Banded Horn Brewing in Biddeford, Maine, does an excellent version called Green Warden. Yes, indeedy, hops play well with spruce. We have also brewed with old spruce cones, even some that were on the ground for a while. While we always prefer fresh-off-the-tree stuff, these oldies are goodies, adding a woody funk and sour tinge to a pale gruit that had pine boughs and yarrow. We will certainly be doing more cone brews in the future.

As discussed previously, when foraging, be respectful and responsible. Much better to take a few tips off many trees than to clip them all off the same tree and significantly stunt its growth. Oh, and if you're not going to use them right away, bag and toss 'em in your freezer. The sooner you freeze them after picking, the longer they will keep—up to a year.

CONNIE FERALE

YIELD: 5 GALLONS (18.9 L), ALL-GRAIN

9 lb (4 kg) 2-row

1.25 lb (567 g) amber

1 lb (454 g) white wheat

9.2 oz (260 g) melanoiden

9.2 oz (260 g) flaked oats

9.2 oz (260 g) pale chocolate

5.3 oz (150 g) crystal 60

Total Grain Bill: 13.25 lb (6 kg)

Mash Water: 4.17 gallons (15.8 L)

Sparge Water: 4 gallons (15 L)

Mash Temperature: 151°F (66°C)

Mash Time: 60 minutes

Sparge Water Temperature: 168°F (76°C)

Boil Time: 60 minutes

HERBS , ETC.*

2.4 oz (68 g) ½ @ 30 minutes, ½ @ flame-out chaga (processed)

3.2 oz (90 g) ½ @ 5 minutes, ½ @ post-fermentation spruce tips (chopped)

3.2 oz (90 g) ½ @ 15 minutes, ½ @ post-fermentation pine candles (chopped)

YEAST

Any Scottish or British ale yeast

Target OG: 1.064

Target FG: 1.015

ABV: 6.4%

You'll need to prep the chaga into two bags (see Chaga Groove, page 54). For further extraction, you may want to add the second addition chaga bag to your fermenter. Your tips and candles will need some tender loving care too, as my relatives in Louisiana say, to "get the goodie." I like to use a food processor on brew day, but chopping them up finely with a good knife will certainly work. After you break them down, bag half and toss back into the freezer—you'll need 'em in a week or so for some "dry-tipping."

About ten days after brewing, draw off a quart (1 L) or so of the beer and gently whisk in the remaining tips and candles. Stretch a bag over a clean pitcher and pour the mix into it. You'll want to add the bag as well as the strained beer back to your fermenter.

Note: Amounts are for dried herb. If fresh, double the amounts. Cut up the leaf and flowers, place in a muslin bag and bruise the herb by squeezing and rubbing the bag vigorously.

TASTING NOTES

Brewer's Note: *Dark colored but not heavy bodied. Rich and roasty with slight coffee and dark caramel. Maltiness hides 7.4% alcohol. Perfect amount of spruce flavor, brown sugar, flowers, some fermented fruit but not bitter; touch of sweetness. Chewy light body.*

ONLINE BEER REVIEWS

Untappd.com Members

"Rich and roasty; light pine flavor but not bitter; touch of sweetness; tasty."

"Lots of flowery flavors. Chewy body. Weird and tasty."

"Proper gruit. Perfect amount of spruce, which I say because I used spruce essence in a home brew 20 years ago and failed."

"Good ass beer. You can really taste the pine and spruce."

"Flavors of brown sugar, flowers and a touch of fermented fruit. Light body."

"Sprucy but a little too malty."

"Roasty, smooth and full of flavor!"

"Delectable. Maltiness that hides the alcohol, slight coffee, dark caramel flavor."

BIRTHDAY BOY

This beer was first brewed in mid-May, which turned out to be the Buddha's birthday that year. It's a light yet flavorful brew and all the ingredients can be foraged around this time. Although we've done a few worthy iterations with different herb blends, the constant has been to brew an expression of this particular season—full on spring.

Burdock (*Arctium lappa*) grows in almost every ditch, vacant lot and roadside across North America. The challenge is to find it growing in a place other than these sites, as they are all apt to have pollutants in the soil. They can grow more than three feet (0.9 m) tall and have large, broad, smooth-edged leaves. Its most recognizable feature is the flower heads, which have burrs or bristles that cling to clothing and fur with a vengeance—and are said to be the inspiration for velcro. What an effective seed dispersal method! Many sources hail burdock as a blood purifier because it bolsters liver function and as a result is also very helpful with skin issues. It "helps restore the primal blueprint of health . . . when it has been lost in persons suffering from long, chronic illnesses," according to Wood. All parts of the plant are useable; however, we are after the roots, which will require some effort to harvest. They lend an earthy, somewhat spicy flavor akin to green peppers.

Not quite as easy to find, but still out there, are flowers and leaves of the motherwort plant (*Leonurus cardiaca*). This is one bitter herb, right up there with wormwood and horehound, especially when dried. It's great stuff in small amounts, but a brew-wrecker if overdone. We got a bit liberal with it in a different beer recently and had to offer the whole batch up to the drain gods. The early Greeks gave motherwort to pregnant women suffering from anxiety, hence the name motherwort, or "mother's herb," according to Susun Weed. In North America, the Cherokees used it as a sedative as well. Weed mentions "an old tale about a town whose water source was a stream flowing through banks of motherwort." Many of the townspeople lived to be 130 years old and recall one who reportedly lived to 300 years. "Old writers tell us that there is no better herb for strengthening and gladdening the heart," reported Grieve. Curiously, in the *Victorian Language of Flowers*, motherwort symbolizes concealed love.

Mugwort (*Artemisia vulgaris*) is one of those quintessential brewing herbs, as reflected in its name. We have used it in many different brews over the years, and its particular bitter herbal taste plays well with malt flavors of all kinds. It grows in the usual weedy places like roadsides and disturbed soils. Although we've used it green, most sources agree that the flower tops and leaves should be dried before use. "Malt liquor was then boiled with it so as to form a strong decoction, and the liquid thus prepared was added to the beer," Grieve offers. This is the first English reference that I've come across that points to a newly re-discovered iteration of gruit. Brewer-historian Fredrick Ruis contends that in sixteenth-century Netherlands, England and perhaps some Nordic countries, gruit referred to a malt extract in which herbs were boiled. This herbed extract was then sold to brewers to add to their ales from the "Gruithuis," or gruit house.

Mugwort has a long history in herbalism primarily to help with female health issues. Wood cited Susun Weed, who maintains that it strengthens feminine instincts such as intuition and creativity in both men and women. Mugwort eases anxiety, helps sleep and aids digestion as a bitter, and is said to promote dreaming, particularly when smoked. "Completed and current ongoing studies on the possible uses of mugwort indicate that links to the fundamental component of the plant, artemisinins, as being toxic to certain cancer cells. Relatedly, mugwort is a naturally occurring anti-malarial," Dr. Josh Axe reported on his website. If you have worms, mugwort will kill 'em too.

You won't find much info out there if you search for spruce flowers. While Jenna Darcy, our forager, swears the term is legit, other experts maintain they've never heard of such a thing. Regardless, the immature cones of the spruce tree are what we are talking about here, and they are fantastic! They appear in May and June, and have a pinkish purple hue. Keep in mind that evergreens in general are rather erratic in their cone production, perhaps because of climate fluctuations, so there's no guarantee that you will find any in a given season. If you do, rejoice. Can't find any? Pine pollen cones are a great substitute/addition. These are the small male cones that also appear in the spring, the ones responsible for covering New England in yellow pollen dust. Harvesting just before they release is ideal, but getting them during will work. If you are allergic this could be dicey, however once used in a beer the pollen seems to lose its irritating qualities. Rich in testosterone, these little guys define fertility in the forest.

BIRTHDAY BOY

YIELD: 5 GALLONS (18.9 L), ALL-GRAIN

9.06 lb (4.11 kg) Belgian pilsner
1.16 lb (526 g) Vienna
5.3 oz (150 g) crystal 40
Total Grain Bill: 10.55 lb (4.79 kg)

Mash Water: 3.29 gallons (12.45 L)
Sparge Water: 4.47 gallons (16.92 L)

Mash Temperature: 151°F (66°C)
Mash Time: 60 minutes
Sparge Water Temperature: 168°F (76°C)
Boil Time: 60 minutes

HERBS , ETC.*
1 oz (28 g) @ 30 minutes burdock root (processed)
2 oz (56 g) ½ @ flame-out (f/o), ½ after primary spruce flowers (processed)
1 oz (28 g) @ flame-out (f/o) motherwort
1 oz (28 g) @ flame-out (f/o) mugwort

Past versions: sweet fern, pine pollen cones, yarrow

YEAST
Brettanomyces Lambucus or Ardennes

Target OG: 1.050
Target FG: 1.011
ABV: 5.1%

Per usual, getting the goodie involves maximizing surface area. Chop up those burdock roots and spruce flowers as much as possible, and using a food processor will save some time. Split the flowers between two bags and toss one in the freezer. You'll add that second bag, with a weight, to your fermenter after primary is complete in a week or so. Again, be sure to knot bags close to the opening so as to create maximum volume in it. Usual drill with the herbs: cut up or break up in a roomy container, bag and then bruise them up good—rubbing and crushing the bag.

Note: Amounts are for dried herb. If fresh, double the amounts. Cut up the leaf and flowers, place in a muslin bag and bruise the herb by squeezing and rubbing the bag vigorously.

TASTING NOTES

Brewer's Note: *Pours golden with a medium carbonation. Aroma is very earthy and herbal with pine, spruce and flowers. Flavor is more mellow. Fleeting herbal-ness, green pepper grassiness, tangy tartness. Mouthfeel is nice and smooth with a medium body. Easy drinking.*

ONLINE BEER REVIEWS

BeerAdvocate.com Members

"This is one of the most unique beers I have ever tasted in my life. The smell is incredibly earthy . . . like literally almost smelling earth.

The taste? This is the earthiest and most unique flavor I have ever had out of a beer. It's got the earthiness and grassiness of a green pepper, but in the best way possible. Very unique. Pairs very well with BBQ."

Untappd.com Members

"Like nothing I've tasted before!"

"My first gruit. Earthy, lightly sour. Complex."

"Nice mouthfeel."

"Tastes like the fruits of the earth."

CONTINUING THE ADVENTURE

HERBAL AFFAIRS

This book has presented just a tiny selection of the plants that can be used in brewing. The work of discovering, tasting, blending and brewing has already been done for each recipe here, but I encourage you to continue to develop them into something that is uniquely yours. To my mind, everything I have presented with these twelve beers is interchangeable and fluid. I encourage you to mix and match ingredients to your heart's content! Even more so, I hope you will be moved and empowered to explore more of the plant world, particularly the flora that is local to you. Here are some suggestions on how to begin working with herbs, including the ones mentioned in this book.

Once you have established the safety and ingestibility of a plant via local experts and book and/or online research, it becomes a matter of flavor. I'm familiar with three methods of acquainting oneself with an herb. The first is to infuse a glass of neutral beer with a good pinch of the herb, stir it up, let it sit for a bit and then have a taste. If you aren't tasting much, let it sit longer or put a bit more herb in the beer. Another is to make some tea. Put some of the bruised or otherwise processed plant in a cup, pour some boiling water over it, let it steep and then sip.

The method I often default to is the "sniff 'n' chew." For the fresh stuff, I'll crumple some of it between my fingers and rub it a bit—and inhale. For dried, I'll give a bag of herbs a shake, open it and very slowly breathe in a bit of the dust. Careful, though; if you take too strong a pull, it can kick off some amazing sneezing fits. I have been graced with dust allergies and I have actually kicked off attacks doing this with too much vigor. Next, I'll take a very small amount in my mouth, chew it a bit and let my saliva hydrate it. I'll try and wait a few seconds before I really start to tune into the taste.

Regardless of the method you choose (try them all!), the challenge is to get past whether or not you like that particular flavor and instead really consider whether it will be good in a beer. This means you'll also need to think of what style of beer it might be best in. Write your thoughts down, record what you are tasting and start to build your own personal herbal index. There are lots of flavor wheels out there—a great help for expanding your tasting vocabulary.

Once you've experienced each plant individually, it's time to investigate some blending. Mix equal parts in your beer or tea and see what you think. Adjust the amounts and try it again. If you're doing the sniff 'n' chew, get a whiff of each herb in succession. Mix up a tiny pinch and see what your mouth has to say. In her fascinating book on perfume called *Fragrant: The Secret Life of Scent*, Mandy Aftel described "scent registers," clearly relevant to developing new flavors by combining herbs. Top or head notes are the first scents to register on the nose and the first to fade. Middle or heart notes show up next and linger a bit longer whilst the base notes bring up the rear and last the longest.

Coriander, spearmint, ginger, black pepper, cardamom and basically herbs and spices we know from cooking are good examples of top notes, according to Aftel. For middle notes, largely floral scents, which she described as giving body, warmth and fullness to blends, include rose, jasmine, lavender, cinnamon and nutmeg. On base notes, roots, bark, resins, grasses and animal essences are good examples, according to Aftel. These are the intense, profound, thick and syrupy flavors. I present this not as a dogmatic formula, but as a loose framework around which to think about herbs and their blending. These three registers are always in the back of my mind when experiencing new flavors and contemplating new blends.

And now the caveat: These methods may or may not indicate how your beer will be affected—it varies wildly with each herb and herb blend. Sometimes the flavors you experience carry straight through to the finished product; other times they don't; and yet other times, the flavors have morphed into something else. It's either tremendously frustrating or endlessly exciting—often a combination. There are likely some very exact and technical ways to quantify such information that the big breweries have access to, but we are over here on the artsy/intuitive side of the spectrum. I believe one's personal experience is far more valuable than the results of some machine's chemical analysis—but that's just me.

Wild cherry   *Always with the stripping*

THE MICROSCOPIC MASTERS

Don't forget our other brew partners—yeast! As you know, it's quite literally all over the place, in the air, on every surface, all over you and all over plants. The cool thing is that all of it can ferment your beer because all yeast consumes sugar. Obviously, some yeasts yield better-tasting beer than others and we're all familiar with the relatively few strains that have been domesticated and packaged for sale. It so happens that wild fruit is covered with just the right yeast strains to ferment the sweetness underneath its skin. Don't take my word for it—mash some wild unwashed berries up, mix them into some sugar water or wort, put it in a fementer and let it rip for three or four weeks. Just strain and drink. We've also used these impromptu starters on occasion to ferment our gruits—with great results.

Some herbs carry particularly interesting strains, many of which have likely not been discovered yet. An interesting example is heather. I have yet to experience this, but I have read that along the moors of Britain, the native heather is covered with a white powdery yeast or mildew locally called fogg. Likely a combination of different flora, not only is it known to ferment beer well, it supposedly contributes psychoactive properties to a beer or mead made with it.

What I'm driving at here is that truly wild yeast absolutely warrants investigation and experimentation. There are breweries around the world focusing on beer made with yeast they have personally captured and propagated—and anyone can do it. Whether you use microscopes and petri dishes or just wing it as we do on occasion, growing up whatever is on the given plant matter by plopping it in a fermenter with some fresh wort, yeast can provide an even deeper experience and expression of terroir, of your time and your place.

BECOME YOUR OWN EXPERT, PLEASE!

We've become so dependent on "experts" and the "authorities," on the facts and preconceptions of others, that our own urges to explore and our abilities to perceive have all but disappeared—and that's a tragedy. Our lives are spent in electric cocoons that "protect us" from the scary chaotic outside. Shielded from the sun, the wind, rain and snow, we are effectively hiding from the environment we were meant to live in. As we drift further and further from our real world, we lose track of what's important, and what's necessary for our survival. The climate continues to warm, water and air continue to be polluted, our oceans fill up with plastic and trash, and species after species of plant and animal become endangered and extinct. Multinational corporations are patenting seeds and genetically altering plants, bees and bats are on the decline . . . I could go on.

We brewers will be among the first to know when we've finally wrecked all the natural systems that keep us alive because again, brewing is a plant-dependent pursuit—no farms, no food. But it will be too late unless we get out of our electric cocoons and look beyond the "experts," and get some direct experience of our own. Only then we can truly understand and appreciate the world around us, just as the first humans did millennia ago.

So take a big bounce off of this paper diving board and cultivate some raw experience that is absolutely yours, not only with the natural world, but with brewing too. It is my sincere hope that you will have experiences with plants and brewing that will eventually take you beyond what myself and others have presented. I urge you to embrace the responsibility we all are tasked with to look beyond and beneath and between the supposed facts and rules, so that you can effectively create your own. Remember and honor those who came before us, the so-called primitive and uncivilized peoples who survived and thrived in direct relationship with the earth—a relationship of cooperation and balance rather than exploitation and domination. Whether you're brewing botanical beer or consciously drinking it, cooking with botanicals or attentively eating them, foraging or farming or just admiring and appreciating plants, you'll be on your way to becoming your own expert.

MASTER LIST

Here's a list of almost all of the plants we've successfully brewed with so far:

- Agave
- Alehoof
- Angelica
- Anise
- Apple
- Autumn Olive
- Balsam
- Barberry
- Barley
- Basil
- Bay
- Beach Plum
- Beans
- Beech
- Beet
- Betony
- Birch
- Blackberry
- Black Locust
- Black Trumpet Mushroom
- Blessed Thistle
- Blood Oranges
- Blueberries
- Blue Vervain
- Brahmi

- Broom
- Buckthorn
- Buckwheat
- Burdock
- Cacao
- Catnip
- Calamus
- Calendula
- California Poppy
- Caraway
- Cardamom
- Chaga Mushroom
- Chamomile
- Chasteberry
- Cherry
- Cherry, Wild
- Chickweed
- Chili Pepper
- Chocolate
- Chokeberry
- Cinnamon
- Clary Sage
- Cleavers
- Coconut
- Coffee
- Coltsfoot

- Coriander
- Corn
- Crabapples
- Cranberry
- Curry
- Damiana
- Dandelion
- Dates
- Dock
- Dogwood
- Echinacea
- Elderberry
- Fennel
- Fig
- Fir
- Galangal
- Garlic Mustard
- Gentian
- Ginger
- Glasswort
- Gooseberry
- Grains of Paradise
- Grape, Wild/Feral
- Grape Root
- Ground Ivy
- Hawthorn

Autumn Olives

Blueberry

Cleavers

Beans

Blue Vervain

Crabapples

Beech Leaf

Black Cherry

Dogwood Berries

Wild Grapes

Lamb's Quarters

Rose Hips

Wild Grapes

Nannyberry

Spicebush

Ground Ivy

Wild Carrot (Queen Ann's Lace)

Sumac

- Heather
- Hibiscus
- Honey
- Hops
- Horehound
- Hyssop
- Irish Moss
- Japanese Knotweed
- Juneberries
- Juniper
- Kamut
- Kava Kava
- Labrador Tea
- Lamb's Quarters
- Lavender
- Lemon
- Lemon Balm
- Lemon Grass
- Lemon Verbena
- Lettuce, Wild
- Licorice
- Lilac
- Lime
- Linden
- Lungwort
- Mace
- Maitake Mushroom (Hen of the Wood)
- Mandrake
- Maple
- Marjoram
- Marshmallow

- Meadowsweet
- Melon, various
- Mistletoe
- Molasses
- Motherwort
- Mountain Ash
- Mugwort
- Muira Puama
- Mustard
- Myrtle
- Nannyberry
- Nutmeg
- Oat
- Parsnips
- Passion Fruit
- Pau d'Arco
- Pear
- Pennyroyal
- Peppers, various
- Pine
- Pineapple Weed
- Plantain, Broadleaf
- Poplar
- Privet Fruit
- Prune
- Queen Anne's Lace
- Raisin
- Raspberry
- Rhubarb
- Rice
- Rose Hips
- Rosemary, Wild

- Rye
- Sage
- Sarsaparilla
- Sassafras
- Schisandra Berry
- Sea Blight
- Sea Rocket
- Shepherd's Purse
- Skullcap
- Sorrel
- Spearmint
- Speedwell
- Spicebush
- Spikenard, American
- Spruce
- Squash, various
- Star Anise
- Stinging Nettles
- St. John's Wort
- Strawberry
- Sumac
- Sweet Fern
- Sweet Gale
- Tea, Various
- Wintergreen
- Wormwood
- Yarrow
- Yerba Santa
- Yohimbe

RESOURCES

BOOKS

Aftel, Mandy, *Fragrant: The Secret Life of Scent*. New York, NY: Riverhead Books. 2014

Bamforth, Charles, *Beer: Tap into the Art and Science of Brewing*. New York, NY: Oxford University Press. 2009

Baudar, Pascal, *The New Wildcrafted Cuisine*. White River Junction, VT: Chelsea Green Publishing Company. 2016

Bennett, Judith M., *Ale, Beer and Brewsters in England*. New York, NY: Oxford University Press. 1996

Buhner, Stephen Harrod, *Sacred Plant Medicine*. Rochester, VT: Bear & Company. 1996

Buhner, Stephen Harrod, *Sacred and Herbal Healing Beers*. Boulder, CO: Brewers Publications. 1998

Buhner, Stephen Harrod, *Plant Intelligence and the Imaginal Realm*. Rochester, VT: Bear & Company. 2014

Calagione, Sam, *Extreme Brewing*, Gloucester, MA: Quarry Books. 2006

Cornell, Martyn, *Amber Black & Gold, History of Britain's Great Beers*. Gloucestershire, UK: The History Press. 2010

Dornbusch, Horst, *Beer Styles from Around the World*. West Newbury, MA: Cervisia Communications. 2015

Fischer, Joe, and Fischer, Dennis, *The Homebrewer's Garden*. North Adams, MA: Storey Publishing. 1998

Grieve, Mrs. M., *A Modern Herbal*. New York, NY: Dover Publications, Inc. 1931

Hieronymus, Stan, *Brewing Local*. Boulder, CO: Brewers Publications. 2016

Hutton, Ronald, *The Triumph of the Moon*. New York, NY: Oxford University Press. 1999

Jackson, Michael, *Michael Jackson's Beer Companion*. Philadelphia, PA: Running Press Book Publishers. 1993

Josephson, Marika, Kleidon, Aaron, and Tockstein, Ryan, *The Homebrewer's Almanac*. New York, NY: The Countryman Press. 2016

Katz, Sandor Ellix, *Wild Fermentation*. White River Junction, VT: Chelsea Green Publishing Company. 2003

McGovern, Patrick E., *Uncorking the Past*. Berkeley, CA: University of California Press. 2009

Mosher, Randy, *Radical Brewing*. Boulder, CO: Brewers Publications. 2004

Oliver, Garret, *The Oxford Companion to Beer*. New York, NY: Oxford University Press. 2012

Pendell, Dale, *Pharmako Poeia, Power Plants, Poisons & Herbcraft*. Berkeley, CA: North Atlantic Books. 1995

Pendell, Dale, *Beer: A History of Suds and Civilization from Mesopotamia to Microbreweries*. New York, NY: Avon Books. 1995

Pendell, Dale, *Pharmako Dynamis, Stimulating Plants, Potions & Herbcraft*. Berkeley, CA: North Atlantic Books. 2002

Pendell, Dale. *Pharmako Gnosis, Plant Teachers and the Poison Path*. Berkeley, CA: North Atlantic Books. 2005

Purkiss, Diane, *The Witch in History*. London, UK: Routledge. 1996

Schultes, Richard Evans and Hofmann, Albert, *Plants of the Gods*. Rochester VT: Healing Arts Press. 1992

Smith, Greg, *Beer in Early America, The Early Years—1587–1840*. Boulder, CO: Brewers Publications. 1998

Sparrow, Jeff, *Wild Brews: Beer Beyond the Influence of Brewer's Yeast*. Boulder, CO: Brewers Publications. 2005

Tonsmeire, Michael, *American Sour Beers*. Boulder, CO: Brewers Publications. 2005

Unger, Richard, *Beer in the Middle Ages and the Renaissance*. Philadelphia, PA: University of Pennsylvania Press. 2004

Wood, Matthew, *The Earthwise Herbal: A Complete Guide to Old World Medicinal Plants*. Berkeley, CA: North Atlantic Books. 2008

Wood, Matthew, *The Earthwise Herbal: A Complete Guide to New World Medicinal Plants*. Berkeley, CA: North Atlantic Books. 2009

HERBAL SUPPLIERS

It's so easy to shop online, isn't it? A few key strokes and poof! It's sitting on your doorstep. Understand that in this case, the path of least resistance is not the best path. Please consider these healthy and socioeconomical responsible steps before you send your money off to some far-flung company:

1) Get out there and forage for it yourself—it's free.

2) Grow it yourself—it's almost free.

3) Find a professional forager and have them find what you want—it keeps your money local.

4) Visit local farmers' markets and see what's available. They might be interested in growing what you want if they don't have it, or at least know a fellow farmer who might have it—it keeps your money local.

5) Visit your local herb or health food store—it keeps some of your money local, but some of it most likely leaves your area.

If you've tried all of these alternatives and struck out, it's time to send your money off into the wild blue yonder. My wife and I have had good results with the following companies; hopefully some are local to you:

- **Mountain Rose Herbs**—mountainroseherbs.com

- **Monterey Bay Spice Company**—herbco.com

- **Wild Weeds**—wildweeds.com

- **Monteagle Herbs**—monteagleherbs.com

- **Bouncing Bear Botanicals**—bouncingbearbotanicals.com

- **Star West Botanicals**—starwest-botanicals.com

- **Penn Herb Company**—pennherb.com

Keep in mind that there are a wide variety of sources for each of these companies. Some forage and/or grow for themselves, and others import from all over the world from different farms and foragers. Some of their products are certified organic and others are not. Some are processed into different forms and some are sold whole. Take time to familiarize yourself with what these companies offer and how they present—each one is different.

Most of these outlets also sell hops—for much more money and with far less information than the usual brewing-related companies. Not recommended.

CRAFT MALT

If you'd rather not do business with the big corporations and are interested in using local grains, do search for a maltster in your area. Their products will be more expensive, but they are typically higher quality, local varietals. You'll also be keeping your money local.

North American Craft Maltsters Guild—craftmalting.com

ACKNOWLEDGMENTS

To my wife, herbalist April O'Keefe: Thank you for waking me up to the wonderful world of plants by surrounding me with your amazing apothecary, rich library, employing me as your primary guinea pig and taking very good care of me—particularly whilst writing this book!

To my brother-in-law and business partner, Alex McDonald: So glad my sister Gretchen found you and that you and I have been able to co-create this wonderful adventure in beer. Your unconditional support and encouragement are muchly appreciated. Thanks for giving me enough room (rope?) for me to be me.

To "our" forager, Jenna Darcy: I can't thank you enough for being my direct link to a seemingly endless bounty of local flora. Your positive energy, boundless enthusiasm and homesteader spirit has been a constant and powerful inspiration to me. I sincerely hope that everyone who is moved to action by this book finds, or becomes, their own Jenna!

To our employees at Earth Eagle Brewings: Alex and I have been so very fortunate to have you all as part of our team. Thank you for treating our customers so well with great service, artful cooking and bodacious brewing. We could never have done it without you.

To the members of my writers group (Beeotches!): May this be just the first of many published works to emerge from the crucible we have created over the last many years.

Special thanks also to Craig Baskis, Tricia Peone, Will Meyers, Emerson "Tad" Baker, Evan Mallet, Tod Mott, Paul Saylor, Lauren J. Clark and Amy K.S. Sterndale.

To Will Kiester and the team at Page Street Publishing: Thanks so much for making me a real author and creating such a beautiful book!

ABOUT THE AUTHOR

"I am a firm believer in the people. If given the truth, they can be depended upon to meet any national crisis. The great point is to bring them the real facts, and beer."

—Abraham Lincoln

Mid 1970s, Gilford, NH. I was 11 or 12 and my dad had one of his buddies over to watch a game. They were hanging out in the basement drinking Schaefer and Rheingold and probably Narragansett beer. I think my dad might have given me a can, as I was not yet at that alcohol-swiping point in my life. I drank it and vividly remember walking down the driveway with a big grin on my face. I didn't like the taste but gosh it felt good.

Early 1980s, University of New Hampshire. Over the years a hierarchy of beer began to form in my mind and those of my fellow underage drinkers. Heineken was the top of our known world o' beer, with an even higher honor going to Heineken Dark. Keith turned me on to this stuff from Ireland, a thick dark brew, viscous, roasty and smooth that seemed more like a meal than a beer. Guinness Stout made a big impression on me, and I started drinking it whenever I could procure it.

Early 1990s, New York City. Christina took me to a bar in the East Village called Burp Castle. The waitstaff were dressed as monks and medieval drinking scenes adorned the walls above a line of big, rugged picnic tables. There I experienced my first Belgian beer and boom! my taste buds went on a roller-coaster ride I've never recovered from! God bless you, Christina! That same year Bill shared a beer with me that had an enjoyable bitterness that was quite foreign to me. Looking back I realize this beer, Harpoon IPA created by the venerable Tod Mott, was one of the early beers that launched the current hoppy beer craze.

April O'Keefe and I married in 2003. A budding herbalist, I was struck by her belief that plants are our allies, living beings here to help us. I read *Sacred and Herbal Healing Beers*, written by one of April's herbal heroes, Stephen Harrod Buhner. Suddenly an exciting and dynamic connection emerged between April's herbal endeavors and my interest in beer. Discovering gruits and then contemplating an infinite array of beers from infinite combinations of herbs, roots, bark, fruit and mushrooms was wholly intoxicating—and motivating. It was after reading *The Art of Fermentation* by Sandor Katz that I began to feel like I could really brew beer. Katz provided a reassuring "anyone can do this" ethos along with a deep reverence for the microscopic life-forms who conduct the real alchemy of brewing: fermentation.

2008 and my sister Gretchen meets Alex, they begin to see each other, and eventually Alex and I find we have lots of interests in common: music, spirituality and good beer, to name a few. I told him I was going to start home brewing and asked if he wanted in. Turned out he had brewed a few times years ago and was keen to get back into it. We started brewing in a turkey fryer perched on the picnic table in my back yard—and we were off!

I don't remember a particular moment when the idea of starting a brewery was hatched. I came across a flock of wild turkeys on the way to a brew day and Alex mentioned that some Native Americans refer to wild turkeys as "eagles of the earth." Then the band-name moment came: Earth Eagle! The term "brewings" came up pretty quick thereafter. It sounded a tad mysterious, more like witches huddled over a kettle than a beer factory. And we certainly didn't want to give our friends and families blank bottles of beer with cryptic initials on the caps, so we began to think up pithy names and designed labels with our newly hatched brewery name and logo. I guess we started playing faux brewery as soon as we had beer we were proud to share.

We continued to brew about once a week and had created some good recipes, as evidenced by the little collection of home brew medals we were winning. Alex started thinking about opening a home brew shop, and after stumbling into a great space he and Gretchen quit their day jobs and took the plunge. In 2010, A&G Homebrew Supply was born. Our brewing acumen grew as we enjoyed access to lots of supplies and equipment—at wholesale prices. Another bonus involves the old adage that the best way to learn is to teach. With Alex suddenly in a brew shop seven days a week, he had to teach it. He read books, magazines and scoured the Internet voraciously—and we continued to brew a new batch every weekend. Family and friends kept telling us that they really liked our stuff and wanted to buy it.

There was space available in the building A&G was housed in, so we snapped it up. Starting off small with our ten-gallon (38-L) brewery felt just right to two guys who'd never worked in a brewery before. Well, at least it did until I had a chat with Gary Bogoff, founder of Berkshire Brewing in Massachusetts and one of the few survivors of the microbrew-bubble in the '80s. When I told him we were planning to open a ten-gallon (38 L) brewery he was incredulous. "Are you fucking kidding me? It'll never work, that's way too small! Go big or go home!" When I bumped into Gary a year or so later it was with great satisfaction that I reported we had taken his advice and purchased a larger brew system. "How big did you go?" he asked. "One barrel!" I proudly exclaimed. He just smiled and shook his head.

On November 17, 2012, we opened Earth Eagle Brewings. Alex was full time and I was the weekend warrior. He had successfully lobbied our state government to create a "nanobrewery" license and we were selling 6-ounce (177-ml) pours for a dollar out of our twenty-person tasting room. We were dying to serve a proper pint, which you can't do in NH without serving food, so we eventually shoe-horned in a little kitchen too.

In 2013 we bought some brew kettle sleeves and doubled our output. We brewed on that two-barrel system about three times a week and produced just enough beer to keep the taps pouring—no bottles, no cans and no distribution. When I started noticing the darkening rings under Alex's eyes I knew it was time for me to leave the day job and join him full time—and I was ready.

2016—Three years later Alex and I manage a five-barrel brew house, a 45-seat restaurant and a talented staff of twelve. As I write, we are in the midst of yet another expansion, this time to meet increasing demand for our beer in bars and restaurants throughout Northern New England. What a ride! We are extremely grateful and humbled to be in this position—we're still pinching ourselves today.

Let Butch know what you think! He welcomes your questions, comments or exploits at butch@eartheaglebrewings.com

INDEX